AF324705

# The Switzer Group

EDIZIONI PRESS

# Design as an Understanding of the Business Environment:

# The Switzer Group

First published in the
United States of America by
Edizioni Press, Inc.
469 West 21st Street
New York, New York 10011
Mail@edizionipress.com

ISBN: 0-9662230-5-5

Library of Congress Catalogue Card Number: 00-104799

Printed in Italy

Design and Composition: Claudia Brandenburg

Editorial Director: Anthony Iannacci
Editorial Assistants: Jenny Kwok, Jamie Schwartz, Kara Janeczko

# Lou Switzer: A Life in Design
## By Peter Slatin

Even before Lou Switzer journeyed north to New York City from South Carolina more than 30 years ago, he knew what he wanted to do once he arrived: design spaces and places for the better.

At age 17, Switzer did not yet understand fully what that meant; but at that time, in the late 1960s, he had plenty of company. Indeed, the profession of interior design was not much older than he was himself, and it too was struggling to earn respect and make a name for itself. In much the same way, the young profession and the young man were finding their ways in the world around them. In doing so, as we well know, they also found each other. For each, that discovery of self and of self-worth has proved a splendid accommodation.

Now, more than a quarter century after setting up his own practice, Lou Switzer can survey his achievement to date from the comfort of a favorite rocking chair in his spacious office in a Fifth Avenue skyscraper. His firm, The Switzer Group, Inc., is firmly established among the top ranks of interior design firms in design and in billings, and has field offices in Washington, D.C., Miami, Florida, and Atlanta, Georgia, as well as Manhattan headquarters. In the late 1990s, the Switzer practice was thriving. They had become the chosen office interiors designer for such corporate giants as The Equitable and Pfizer, Inc.. They had also designed executive suites for Phillips-Van Heusen and state-of-the-art training facilities for Consolidated Edison, the nation's largest electric utility company.

Those projects and many more are laid out in their stunning variety and imaginative ambition throughout this volume, where the strong thread that links them one to another is in ample evidence. That thread is simplicity: The Switzer Group, Inc. projects are marked by their full embrace of handsome form directly expressed in flowing surfaces that, no matter what the environment they are found in, are rich, warm and always human.

The Switzer (pronounced SWI-tzer) story is one that Lou himself now delights in telling: how as a young man he was drawn north to the urban center of America, driven by his own talent and by the necessity of providing for two infants and a young wife. How he found work through perseverance and determination. How that hard work paid off as he moved quickly ahead. How his abilities and energies allowed the young African-American to thwart the subtle and sublimated negative impulses of the age as he continued to grow professionally and personally.

Yes, Lou Switzer delights in telling his story. But that he does so is not evident in his voice, which betrays neither unwanted pride nor spite—for he appears to bear none. Instead, it is his straightforward delivery that, in its even detailed recounting, reveals how justly proud he is of the journey he has taken—and the one on which he continues—because it is clearly a trail he blazed for himself, sometimes with the help of others, sometimes on his own.

"My dream was always to become an architect, ever since the fourth grade," Switzer recalls one morning in his spotless and smart—and classically Switzer—office, fitted with a plush sofa and other chairs less severe than the battered wooden rocker into which Switzer has settled. "My aunt's husband was an architect, and I used to watch him. When I saw what he did, the renderings, they were so beautiful. Everything I did from then on stemmed from my aspiration to become an architect." In grade school and in high school, he took art classes and studied mechanical drawing, all geared to fulfilling the imaginative longings of an awestruck nine-year-old.

Those boyhood dreams had evolved a bit by 1975, when as a young man nearing 30 he started his own firm in a 1,000-square-foot penthouse office in a small building at 16 East 52nd Street. "I really had aspirations of building a firm of about six people," he says, letting a soft chuckle escape. "I opened the doors with a secretary and myself. The penthouse had the most wonderful skylight- you could look out over 52nd North between the buildings." He outgrew the space in a few short years, and sold the lease to menswear designer Alan Flusser. Switzer moved to 3,000 square feet high above Madison Avenue and 53rd Street. Two years later, as the Eighties dawned, he moved his still-growing firm back to 16 East 52nd Street, where he leased 6,000 square feet. In three more years, the firm busted out of midtown Manhattan—to 16,500 square feet downtown at 902 Broadway, in an area of Manhattan on the edge of hip—and far more affordable than Switzer's previous locations. He employed 85 people.

That office held The Switzer Group, Inc. for the next decade. As the recession-wracked early years of the Nineties took hold, Switzer made the critical strategic decision to move in order to position the firm and its space efficiently, relocating to 11,000 square feet in 535 Fifth Avenue at 44th Street, where it has remained since. "I went from my hoping to have six people to having 85, but when we had 85 employees, it didn't work for us," he says. Faced with a decision to continuously grow to a size he felt uncomfortable with or to shrink back to a more manageable level, Switzer chose the latter, acknowledging the twin pressures of increasing technology and what was then an unknown economic outlook. Switzer resolved to limit his staff to 50—and to remain at that level, using the leverage of technology to foster growth.

That decision has served Lou Switzer and his firm well. It is emblematic of a strong understanding of business practice as well as of a powerful management ability that has propelled him to mastery of the intertwined minefields of Manhattan's design, construction and real estate industries.

# The Journey

It is what happened in the decade before he ever signed his first lease on East 52nd Street in 1975 that compels us to wonder at what brings a person and a career onto the right path at the right time. For Lou Switzer, the combination of tenacity and ambition—and focus—gained him a foothold into the world he had envisioned as his rightful place—yet a place where he still sounds a bit surprised to find himself. "I must admit, I wasn't a great student per se," he says. "Still, after high school, I decided that I wanted to move to New York to look for my dream."

That's the start of the story. Having made it North—to Brooklyn—and armed with only a high school degree and a portfolio of school shop drawings, he began looking for a job "in the architectural profession" in the City of Churches. He found work—a supermarket job. "I had Thursdays off. But you can't go looking for a job on a Thursday. Monday was the right day. So I would swap with someone on Mondays and go to the state employment office in Brooklyn." An enterprising strategy, yes, but also a good introduction to northern bureaucracy. "I was told, 'Wait a second, we don't have those kinds of jobs in Brooklyn, you have to go to New York City for those.' "

Off he went to the state employment office in Manhattan. "They said, 'You live in Brooklyn, you have to go to Brooklyn.' " Switzer did what many other job seekers have done and still do: called up a friend in Manhattan for permission to use his mailing address. Back he went to the state employment office with proof of a new Manhattan address: "I want something in this field," he insisted.

Persistence paid off. "I got this telegram a week later, saying there's this design firm at 101 Park Avenue"—then known as the Architects' Building—"that needs some help.

Switzer hit the phones and made an appointment. "I said, gee, I've gotta go," remembers Switzer. "I went over the next day, met this very distinguished guy. I probably wear braces now because I was so impressed by this guy and the way he was dressed." Switzer had brought along his portfolio of the drawings he had done in high school, and proudly showed them off to the man in suspenders. "He said, 'That's very nice, but the position we have is for an office boy'—as they called us back then, clerk, mailroom, whatever—'it's only paying $55 a week.' I said, 'that's great, I'll take it.' He said. 'I like that: you'll take it. I haven't offered it yet, but you'll take it. Well, if you want the job, it's yours.' "

The teenager got working papers and started. "Quite frankly, timing is everything," Switzer states brusquely—and then he quickly amends his statement. "It's not just timing," he adds, "but also someone believing in you and having faith and confidence in you."

That message clearly got through to the young Switzer, who today is deeply involved in the work being done at all levels at his firm. Starting each morning at 7:45, he makes several passes through the studio, a ritual that has become known in-house as "Lou's Walking Tour." "All day long, I go from one desk to another," explains Switzer. "I make it my point to communicate with every staff member of this firm, no matter what level, one on one. That open-door policy has tremendously helped this firm—the average stay here is seven years." He is also involved in local mentoring organizations and events, such as the ACE Mentor Program.

But it is the fascinating story of his journey through the ranks of Sherburne & Associates that provides a glimpse of how his diligence and tenacity, combined with opportunity and ability, launched him into his own practice.

At the time—the mid-1960s—the firm was chockablock with work from the burgeoning financial service sector in Wall Street. "Six months into this job as an office boy," recounts Switzer, "they were so busy they needed all the hands they could get to produce the work. And they recalled that I was capable of drawing. So they promoted me to a draftsperson on the boards and"—his voice rising a scant note in pride from its normal soft pitch—"my work was just as good as anybody else's there, if not better." The sudden promotion led to what remains a sweet memory: asked to hire an office boy to fill his old position, he had the pleasure of informing the state employment officer who had helped him earlier that he had moved up the ladder. "She said, 'You're going to hire your replacement?' She just thought it was the greatest thing."

The following three years brought two more events that changed Switzer's life, and that together paint an image of the contradictory social mores and of those disturbing, exciting and challenging times as the nation grappled, often clumsily, with its racial legacy.

Switzer applied to and was accepted by the Pratt Institute in Brooklyn; when he told his boss the good news, the firm's owner called in his bookkeeper to write a check that would cover the $1,000-a-year tuition for Switzer. The support didn't stop there, Switzer recalls. He was put on the owner's every pet project, and allowed the special privilege of working overtime. He was given the keys to his boss's Cadillac convertible while he was on vacation.

Then there was the work itself. For the last two years at the firm, Switzer was the designer for the Atlanta branch of the New York based securities brokerage W.E. Hutton & Co., run by a branch of the same family that ran the more famous and long-lived E.F. Hutton. Although the project had been run out of Manhattan, suddenly, as Switzer tells it, someone needed to be in Atlanta on the job. "Atlanta was a very different city back then," Switzer notes in a passing understatement. "I had worked alone on this particular project for a couple of years, and all of a sudden someone had to go to Atlanta, and all of a sudden I was put as part of a team. I couldn't figure it out—now it's a team effort?"

Something was wrong, he told his new teammate. "I was livid. I suspected why. Someone had to go to Atlanta, but he didn't want to send me."

When Switzer confronted his employer, he offered up Switzer's inexperience as the cause of his team-making decision. The explanation didn't sit well with Switzer, and still doesn't. "I would almost rather he had come out and said, 'Look, I can't send you to Atlanta because of the situation there,' rather than to say, 'you're not experienced,' " Switzer declares. "In any case, I resigned about a month later."

A year later, while working at another interiors firm, Office Design Associates, Switzer got a telephone call. It was from his intended teammate from Sherburne and Associates. He had become the director of facilities planning worldwide for W.E. Hutton & Co., and was calling to ask Lou Switzer to become the company's assistant director of facilities planning. "You're kidding," Switzer told him.

He wasn't. But he had only one request: he wanted Switzer to come to Wall Street for a breakfast meeting with company chief Jim Hutton and himself. "So I went down, had breakfast with him, and Jim [Hutton] came into the meeting. He says 'Hi, I understand you're the guy we're going to hire." Hutton got to the point of the meeting: "What happened between you and your previous employer I knew nothing about. I just wanted you to know this before you accepted this position." Flush with vindication, Switzer took the job and stayed on until the firm closed its doors in 1972.

One more twist to the story stays with Switzer today. When he answered the phone on his first day at Hutton, he heard a familiar voice. "Lee?" he asked an equally surprised Sherburne. " 'Luke?'—they used to call me Luke, I don't know how I allowed that—'Luke, what are you doing there?' " Switzer informed his old boss of his new job, and learned that Sherburne was calling in search of his final paycheck for the Atlanta work. "I've asked accounting to cut a check for you, and you can pick it up this afternoon," Switzer told Sherburne. "That was it."

# In Business

In 1975—after three years trying to make a go of a consulting firm with a partner—Switzer started his own firm at that East 52nd Street office. His "very first" client: Citibank. "We started with a project that was about 80,000 square feet and a fee of $100,000. My very second client was Avon, and the very third was IBM." The Switzer Group is still doing work with those clients today.

# Behind the Work

From the start, what has made Switzer one of the most sought-after designers of corporate interiors is his keen grasp of business and businesses: what they need as well as what they don't. What they need most, he says, is to be understood. For interior designers and architects, understanding is fundamental, he says.

"We've seen the business change drastically over the years," Switzer says of the way design is practiced. But his approach to a job is a constant: "One of the things that helps a project is getting a sense of what their business is all about." From there, the challenge is "how you take their business and create it within the environment you are designing. Your initial conversation is really to get a sense of that," he continues, warming to a theme that is a passion for him. "Know your clients. Know what they are about. Understand what their business is. You don't have to understand how to run that business, but you certainly have to understand the workings of it."

Such understanding, he says, should begin to emerge with initial programming conversations with the client, where the designer can see "how things are attached to each other, how different departments relate to each other, and what is it you're trying to achieve for those various departments." This understanding, Switzer underlines, "is truly the backbone of any great design."

That Switzer truly knows how to work with his clients, from top to bottom, is amply demonstrated by the roster of those that have come back to him again and again in the past quarter century. These include not only IBM and Citibank, but also Consolidated Edison and Chase Bank. But perhaps nothing illustrates his grasp of the essentials of office design more than the work he has done for The Equitable, starting in 1982 and continuing today.

When The Switzer Group, Inc. first took on The Equitable nearly two decades ago, in the early 1980s, the insurance giant was following the management strategies and real estate thinking that prevailed in those early years of the Go-Go decade.

"When we first started doing large projects with The Equitable, it was because they were redeploying people all over the place," Switzer recalls. "At that time, American corporations were splitting their operations up, letting people be responsible for their own P&Ls [profit-and-loss statements]." Following this effort to grant divisions more autonomy and thus greater incentives to be creative, The Equitable moved employees from its headquarters building at 1285 Avenue of the Americas to four separate office locations, three of which were designed by The Switzer Group, Inc. totaling approximately 1 million square feet.

But with the 1990s came a new imperative: consolidation. The Equitable made a smart real estate and management decision. With vacancy high and rents low in Midtown Manhattan, the company leased 550,000 square feet at 1290 Avenue of the Americas—across the street from its namesake headquarters, which it was able to lease out to other tenants as rents had increased.

"It's like a puzzle that you take apart and put back together," muses Switzer about the most recent Equitable project, which was completed a year ago at 1290. "Equitable was a great challenge for us because they were accustomed to very opulent spaces, and that was no longer the corporate image they wanted to portray. So we were given a free hand to create a whole new corporate culture and image for them." The designers had to devise smaller but no less satisfying executive offices, and create uniform work stations for varying grade levels—

not a task guaranteed to win friends. But Switzer was able to pull off the challenge because, he explains, at The Equitable—and at many of his client firms—"the decisions are made from the top down rather from the bottom up. Decisions are made by real decision-makers. And when we are involved with large corporations, that is very, very important."

# Looking Forward

Switzer celebrates the changes in design that have been and are being wrought by the rise of Internet-based businesses, which, he stresses, have brought increased openness and informality to offices and office work. "These companies have allowed us the total freedom of design we didn't have before," Switzer acknowledges. "You see more materials, you see exposed treatments that you try to hide in most corporate environments." The goal, he continues, "is an image that's looser but more creative, yet very functional for the nature of these businesses." Lighting and graphic design—most of which The Switzer Group, Inc. does in-house in order to better control the process—have changed significantly for these tech-heavy businesses. As a result, startup and established new media companies are influencing one another in their approaches to corporate design and management structure, says Switzer. Companies like IBM, where Switzer's firm was deeply involved in the downsizing of Big Blue, "are taking the cues of their own offspring in transforming to nontraditional offices and even to hoteling."

Even as theories about office planning and interior design evolve, The Switzer Group, Inc. continues to create a trademark look for its clients. It is warm and strong, handsome and subdued, never out of sync. Still, says Switzer, returning to one of his favorite themes: "We don't have a trademark per se. It's all specialty. What's really important about what we do is that we try to interpret our clients' goals and objectives and what their needs are. If you look at our projects, you'll notice that each and every project is different, and they are different because they are designed for the specific needs and image requirements of our clients."

That still leads to something recognizable in each setting, a warmth to the work. "That is created by certain materials we believe in. Lighting plays a major role in all of our projects," says Switzer. "And there's always wood somewhere within the pageant."

As the practice moves into its second 25 years, Switzer stays close to the design action, although he remains torn by his need to oversee the management and marketing of the firm's efforts. "I learned a long time ago," he explains reluctantly, "that although my background is in design, if you have a growing business and want to keep it growing, you either have to do it yourself or get someone to do the business part for you. I made the decision to do the business part myself. Though it limits my involvement in the creative process, I made the decision a long time ago."

Focus he has. Nonetheless, whenever possible, he gets his hands dirty in the studio. "There are some projects that I stay close to, because I hate selling some client and then disappearing. I don't disappear. I tell the client, either I'm running this project or someone else is." For example, Switzer took the creation of a new executive office suite and boardroom for Phillips-Van Heusen, from inception "right through to completion of the project."

Along with developing his business, such challenges in design execution are Switzer's true joy. "What gets me going is the excitement of what we do," he declares. "We play a very major role in the business environment, and that role is to create an environment that is effective in its use but that is even more so in terms of the way it gets creative juices flowing when you walk into an office." It's something he has been ahead of his time on since his beginnings—that an enlightening place to work will produce enlightened work. "In the old days, you put people at a desk and you lined them up, rows and rows of desks. Today, it gets a lot deeper—it's the inner workings that are important to any corporation."

Switzer leans forward in his hard rocking chair, which is not rocking. The finished project, he says, is "something you really created from paper and understanding what's on that paper. To see some of those projects can give you goosebumps. It's thrilling and exciting."

# Design as an Understanding of the Business Environment: 25 Years

## 1975

Lou Switzer founds The Switzer Group, Inc. At year's end, the 1,000-square-foot penthouse office on 16 East 52nd Street is filled to full capacity with eight people. IBM and Citibank join the firm's roster of clients. They both continue to provide the firm on-call assignments.

## 1978

Having grown to sixteen employees, The Switzer Group, Inc. relocates to a 3,000-square-foot office on the 31st floor of 515 Madison Avenue.

## 1980

The Switzer Group, Inc. is recognized by *Interior Design* as one of the top 50 giants in the United States. This is a distinction the firm maintains to this date.

## 1982

The Switzer Group, Inc. designs a conference/ display facility for Avon Products, Inc. that is featured in *Interior Design*'s September issue. The project is noted for its glamorous illusory qualities, which reflect Avon's chic image.

Also featured in the September issue of *Interior Design* is Klemptner Advertising, Inc.'s facility, for which the firm relocated 150 persons to 35,000 square feet of space, and the designs for John Alden Life Insurance Company's 12,000-square-foot facility.

For Klemptner Advertising Inc., The Switzer Group, Inc. demonstrates its capabilities by providing impressive, low-cost designs within strict time and budget constraints. Finished in seven weeks time, the corporate workplace is designed to maximize functionality and reflect Klemptner's originality.

Diane von Furstenberg commissions The Switzer Group, Inc. to design offices and showrooms. The architects pay particular attention to color and light, creating a dramatic showcase for clothing.

The Switzer Group, Inc. establishes a satellite office in Baltimore, MD, headed by Elizabeth Holechek, Executive Vice President, and employing a staff of seven.

## 1983

The Switzer Group, Inc. relocates to a larger facility on 16 East 52nd Street.

Coincidentally, it is the same building where the firm started out. In August, this facility is featured in an *Interior Design* article titled "Growth Story." The office houses 30 employees and encompasses 8,000 square feet of space.

Robert T. Sutter, AIA, President, and Stewart Fishbein, Principal, join the firm.

*Interior Design* features the executive dining facility at Bankers Trust in New York.

## 1985

The Equitable Life Assurance Society of the United States' Corporate Operations Facility is featured in the January/February issue of *Corporate Design*.

The Switzer Group, Inc. expands and relocates to 902 Broadway in New York City, occupying 16,500 square feet and employing more than 85 persons.

The Switzer Group, Inc. becomes the first full-service design firm in the country to have an in-house Telecommunications & Information Service Consulting Group: STIS (Switzer Telecommunications & Information Services).

## 1986

Freedom National Bank of New York (located in Brooklyn, New York), wins the 1986 IBD Silver Medal Award and is featured in the November issue of *Interior Design*. The Switzer Group, Inc. renovates the monumental 1930's banking facility. Arched windows provide a dramatic backdrop to the bold interior treatment.

The Switzer Group, Inc. receives The Restaurants and Institutions Award for interior design of The Equitable Life Assurance Society of the United States dining facility at 2 Penn Plaza. For this project, the firm designs 400,000 square feet and relocates 1,200 employees. The Switzer Group, Inc. brings the full weight of its design skills to bear, incorporating functionality and flexibility into a project on a fast-track schedule. This enhances a long-standing relationship with The Equitable.

IBM Corporation retains The Switzer Group, Inc. to assist in the consolidation and relocation of its sales and marketing groups. Working with IBM, the developer, and a work letter, the firm implements creative solutions. Open plan workstations occupy three 45,000-square-foot floors. The design illustrates the sophisticated use of existing corporate standards and an aesthetically pleasing style that softens the rigid base building geometry.

## 1987

The relocation of The Equitable's Investment Management Corporation is featured in the September issue of *Interior Design*. In their design for more than 50,000 square feet of space, the architects create a traditionally designed facility that incorporates specialized computer and trading facilities, as well as a legal library, executive office areas and general office space.

*Manhattan Arts* and *Manhattan Spotlight* feature The Switzer Group, Inc.'s success story and their new corporate office facilities at 902 Broadway.

**1982** Klemptner Advertising, Inc.

**1982** Diane von Furstenberg

**1986** Freedom National Bank of New York

**1987** NYNEX Mobile Communications

# 1988

The May /June issue of *Professional Office Design* features The Switzer Group, Inc.'s new office facility at 902 Broadway.

The Switzer Group, Inc. is engaged by North General Hospital to provide interior design services for a new 270,000-square-foot, eight-story hospital facility. The preparation of a complete furniture and finish package for the entire hospital is an important part of the project.

# 1989

Working with pre-existing NYNEX standards, The Switzer Group, Inc. develops a design for NYNEX Mobile Communications that reflects the corporate synergy synonymous with the communications industry. The design and implementation of the 225,000-square-foot project is carefully coordinated.

# 1990

Gregory Switzer, AIA, (Director of Marketing and Communications) joins the firm.

The Switzer Group, Inc. designs the relocation of Blue Cross Blue Shield of New Jersey's 600,000-square-foot operation center into a new sixteen-story tower in Newark, NJ. A key to the success of the project is the firm's ability to work within a tight time frame and budget constraints. The design consists of a 12,000-square-foot executive area, a corporate cafeteria, a day-care center, a conference and training floor, a fitness center and a customer service area.

# 1991

Consolidating its various groups into one facility, Knight-Ridder Financial Information Services Company calls on The Switzer Group, Inc. to design 150,000 square feet of Wall Street space. The project simplifies a post-modern style and emphasizes the technological aspects of the company's core business.

The Switzer Group, Inc. is involved with the relocation of EMI Music Worldwide to 27,000 square feet of space spread over three floors at Carnegie Hall Tower. The lavish use of materials and furnishings complements the elegant plan, which is interconnected by a sweeping central staircase, accentuating EMI's progressive image as a successful record company.

J. Daniel Mrozek, Senior Associate, joins the firm.

# 1992

For Abbott Capital Management, The Switzer Group, Inc. once again provides a timeless design within rigid time constraints. A quick construction turnaround of eight weeks is critical for this fast growing financial company, but that does not thwart the creation of a sophisticated continuity throughout the office.

The Switzer Group, Inc. is retained by Chase Manhattan Bank to design its MetroTech, Brooklyn corporate dining, training, and central service facilities. Key to the design of this 350,000-square-foot project is the operational program—prepared by The Switzer Group, Inc. during the early stages of the project—and the integration of specialized requirements, such as conveyor, exhaust, and food service systems, which support one of the largest dining facilities in New York, serving over 3,000 persons daily. It is reputed that The Switzer Group, Inc. designed facility serves more hot dogs than Yankee Stadium and Shea Stadium combined.

The design for New Charleston Capital Management was a jewelbox penthouse with panoramic views of the Manhattan skyline, located atop one of the more prestigious buildings in New York City. This is a high-quality traditional space with necessary office technology that is concealed, but readily accessible.

# 1993

Lou Switzer is inducted into the prestigious Interior Design Hall of Fame.

IBM's Regional Headquarters in Cranford, New Jersey is completed and becomes a prototype for "Alternative Officing"/"Free-Address" design. The firm realizes the concept of hoteling. The project is featured in numerous publications including *Interior Design*, *National Officing* (a Japanese Publication), *Business Week*, *The New York Times*, and *Facilities Design and Management*.

The July issue of *Interiors* features EMI Music Worldwide Corporate Facilities. This project is noted for its "...good, solid, timeless design approach."

Consolidated Edison of New York, Inc. commissions The Switzer Group, Inc. to plan and design its new Energy Education Center in Long Island City, New York. Dubbed "The Learning Center," the facility is a 200,000-square-foot state of the art training center for Con Edison employees. The Switzer Group, Inc. assembles and heads the consultant team. This project involves the renovation and expansion of an existing 130,000-square-foot building, which was stripped down to its shell.

Louis Villafañe, Chief Operating Officer, joins the firm.

# 1994

The Switzer Group, Inc. receives an Excellence in Design AIA Award for its design of Consolidated Edison of New York, Inc.'s Learning Center in Long Island City, New York.

Ed Vega, Associate, joins the Switzer Group, Inc.

**1988** Mediators, Inc.

**1991** Knight-Ridder Financial Information Services Company

**1992** Abbott Capital Managament

**1995** The Switzer Group, Inc.

# 1995

Westinghouse Broadcasting commissions The Switzer Group, Inc. to orchestrate the relocation of its 42,000-square-foot facility from Seventh Avenue to 200 Park Avenue. A strong transitional design indicates Westinghouse's ties to the entertainment industry.

The Switzer Group, Inc. relocates to a 10,500-square-foot facility at 535 Fifth Avenue. The firm maintains a staff of 50 people; its office becomes virtually paperless.

Gregory Gresham, RA, Senior Associate, joins the firm.

# 1996

The Switzer Group, Inc. is the recipient of the General Services Administration's Design Award of Honor for its design of the low-rise office interiors at The United States Courthouse at Foley Square in New York City.

# 1997

When Time Warner Telecom separates from its parent company, Time Warner Inc., and moves into a new facility, the company looks to create a distinct identity while still keeping image ties to Time Warner. The Switzer Group, Inc. takes future growth projections and budget constraints into consideration when it outfits the new offices with cherry wood accented by the signature blue Time Warner Telecom logo.

Continuing its long-standing relationship, The Switzer Group, Inc., is again retained by The Equitable (now a subsidiary of French financial giant AXA) to consolidate and relocate more than 550,000 square feet into its current New York City Headquarters at 1290 Avenue of the Americas. The facility consists of seventeen contiguous floors that include executive and general office areas, a data center, computer labs, and a dining facility. The overall design is quite contemporary and incorporates a state of the art technological infrastructure.

*The New York Times* recognizes The Switzer Group, Inc. for its innovative use of computer-animated walk-through for The Equitable executive suites.

# 1998

The Switzer Group, Inc. is featured in *Facilities Design & Management*'s article, "Manhattan Elegance, Silicon Valley Technology," which highlights The Equitable's technology and conferencing facilities. Another article, "Through The Looking Glass," highlights IBM'S Global Services Delivery Center in Melville, New York.

Greenberg Traurig commissions The Switzer Group, Inc. to design its new 82,000-square-foot office facility in the Walter Gropius-designed building (also known in the past as The Pan Am Building and currently called The Met Life Building) at 200 Park Avenue in New York. The interiors for this prestigious Florida-based law firm reflect classic contemporary design.

Pfizer, Inc. commissions The Switzer Group, Inc. to design a corporate dining, training, and amenities center. The architects accentuate the space by using twenty-foot ceilings in the center of the windowless facility. They finish the space with a subtle mixture of materials, including wood, stainless steel, alabaster, and terrazzo.

In pursuit of a New York presence, Allen & Overy, a London based law firm, engages The Switzer Group, Inc. for the fast-track design and construction of its Manhattan office space. The clean traditional design of this facility overlooking the promenade at Rockefeller Center accommodates basic law firm functions, such as private offices, conference areas, and custom administrative workstations.

The Switzer Group, Inc. is engaged by Chase Bank, a longtime client, to design and renovate a 35,000-square-foot space for Chase Manhattan Bank's Securities Lending Facility. Incorporating Chase's existing space standards, the firm maximizes general office space by creatively aligning spaces with the building's axis. The project includes multi-functional conference room facilities and a trading floor.

Western International Media selects The Switzer Group, Inc. to design its 15,500-square-foot New York office facilities. An open office plan, synonymous with new media companies, is utilized throughout the entire office. This concept—in addition to the blue and green wall finishes and the artful use of glass, wood, perforated aluminum ceiling panels and nautical light fixtures—fosters a truly non-hierarchical office environment.

Phillips-Van Heusen, the famed shirt manufacturer, entrusts the design of its 18,000-square-foot executive office space to The Switzer Group, Inc. This facility's design is completed in six weeks to meet Van Heusen's tight schedule.

The Switzer Group, Inc. establishes field office locations in Washington, DC, Atlanta, Georgia, and Miami, Florida.

# 1999

An article published in the premier issue of *Blacklines* highlights the success and philosophy of The Switzer Group, Inc.

The September 1999 issue of *The Network Journal* chronicles The Switzer Group, Inc's's success and features Time Warner Telecom.

Allen & Overy is featured in *Facilities Management & Design*.

# 2000

The Switzer Group, Inc. receives the Prame Studio of the Year Award.

**1995** Westinghouse Broadcasting

**1997** Time Warner Telecom

**1998** IBM Corporation

# Design as an Understanding of the Business Environment:

# The Equitable,
## Re-deployment, various projects 1984-1987

The Equitable refocused its business from insurance to financial services, requiring the decentralization of The Corporate Operations Group and The Life Insurance Group, its two primary operating sectors, and moving the two divisions to more than 250,000 square feet at 40 Rector Street and 400,000 square feet at 2 Penn Plaza, respectively. The Switzer Group, Inc. was commissioned to plan and design these and other spaces, totaling approximately 1 million square feet. Each project was on a fast track.

The program for The Life Insurance Group designated 5,000 square feet for a computer facility and 50,000 square feet for dining and cafeteria spaces. The rest of the interior, almost 90 percent, was open plan, with varying types of managers' offices completing the design; no senior management or executives work at this site. Additional spaces include training, medical and data areas and telecommunications centers. The completed facility housed 1,200 employees. Clever construction management techniques allowed occupancy of the first 100,000 square feet within nine months from the project's inception.

The client wanted this site to include flexible spaces that could be reconfigured as necessary. As a result, the dining and cafeteria complex incorporates spaces suitable for private dining. The entrance to the area is green verde marble, suitable to withstand the heavy traffic. Custom wood paneling lines the walls, while fabric elements help modulate the acoustics. The corporate dining facilities contain a convertible room with panels for dividers. One larger space accommodates as many as 50 people; four smaller rooms can be used for more intimate groups. Maintenance-free materials have been used throughout.

The 20,000-square-foot cafeteria has been arranged with smaller groupings of seatings. Articulated columns help add interest to the expanse. The servery area occupies 2,000 square feet. Soft materials line the walls. The ceramic tile floor is easily cleaned. Restaurants and Institutions presented The Switzer Group, Inc. with its 1986 annual Design Award for Interior Design of The Equitable, 2 Penn Plaza facility.

Entrance hall and elevator lobby, Corporate Operations Group, 40 Rector Street.

The natural light highlights the marble floors in the reception area of the Corporate Operations Group, 40 Rector Street.

The dining room at the Life Insurance Group, 2 Penn Plaza, can be divided by convertible panels to create a more intimate space for smaller meetings.

The Investment Management Corporation's glassed-in conference room is framed by fluted columns and entered via wooden doors, details that add an air of gravitas.

The program for the The Investment Management Corporation, 1221 Avenue of the Americas, stipulated an enormous conference room with all the technological trimmings. This elegant, glassed-enclosed space sits just off the reception area.

A typical investment manager's office at the Investment Management Corporation, 1221 Avenue of the Americas, includes traditional furniture placed in a variety of seating arrangements for formal and casual conversations.

The trading floor of the Investment Management Corporation exhibits columns and pilasters to impart the desired sense of fiduciary responsibility.

The reception area continues this traditional style with its classic furnishings and millwork details.

# Design as an Understanding of the Business Environment:

# Fiat USA, Inc.
## New York, New York 1987

The Switzer Group, Inc. was commissioned to design 7,000 square feet of interior space in the Seagram Building on Park Avenue to house Fiat USA Inc., the U.S. subsidiary of Fiat Italy. The program consisted of a reception area, eight offices, including those for the chairman and president of the U.S. division, and an open plan area for the office support staff.

The Seagram Building, a classic modern office tower designed in the mid 1950s by Ludwig Mies van der Rohe with Philip Johnson, posed a number of challenges, such as working within the building standards for materials. The designers had to detail the new interior in a manner consistent with the character of the building as a whole, and design within certain existing conditions of the space itself: neither the lighting nor the ceiling could be altered.

The Switzer Group, Inc. devised a kind of transcontinental style to suit both Fiat USA, Inc. and the Seagram's envelope. The reception area is appointed with slick, modern Italian furniture and accessories. Walls are highly lacquered, finished like auto bodies. Detail and ornament exemplify the quality of the client's product.

The open-plan area for the support staff makes the most of available
adjacencies, arranging the cubicles directly across the aisle from the private offices.

Details of the interior reveal the
modernist underpinnings of an
interior design derived from the
formal language of the base building,
Mies van der Rohe's and Philip
Johnson's mid-century landmark,
the Seagram Building on Park
Avenue. Three views of the reception
area reveal a highly styled design
solution that encompasses
modern Italian furniture and glossy,
lacquer finishes.

The conference room is appointed with classic modern office furniture, including Herman Miller's Eames-designed aluminum group seating.

Although the designers were prohibited from changing certain standard elements of the space, including the ceiling and overhead lighting fixtures, items like the 20th-century classic Tizio Lamp provided creative solutions.

# Design as an Understanding of the Business Environment:

# Bidermann Industries USA, Inc.
## New York, New York 1989

# Bidermann Industries USA, Inc., the North American license holder

for the Yves Saint Laurent and Daniel Hechter menswear labels, commissioned The Switzer Group, Inc. to design individual showrooms for each licensee. Each showroom occupies its own floor, with direct access a mere step down from the elevator lobby. Each division remains sufficiently separate from the others to ensure clients' privacy. The interior for each licensee also segregates the showrooms from the administrative offices to ensure efficiency as well as privacy. The use of stone on both levels unifies the individual facilities. Each line does, however, have its own distinct materials palette: Yves Saint Laurent is distinguished by stark black and white granite; lighter, muted woods and stone characterize the Daniel Hechter space.

The major difficulty with the Yves Saint Laurent space was the long distance between the elevator lobby and the reception desk. Exaggerating its length proved to be part of the solution. A darkened spotlit ramp forms a granite tunnel that proceeds, like a runway, to the brightly lit and welcoming reception area. Sectioned walls form showroom entrances; two-foot-deep windows ensure the flow of light through the space and protect customer privacy. The showrooms, located off both sides of the reception area, are finished with neutral colors and functional furniture to create quiet environments where the clothes provide the major interest.

Corporate headquarters in Paris prescribed that the interior of the Daniel Hechter showroom should correspond to the rather staid nature of the clothing line. The reception area combines dark wood accents with stone to create a classic, well-appointed space. Color and texture add vitality and contrast to a palette defined by neutrals and earth tones. A screening device of cherry wood rises behind the limestone reception desk; inspired by Japanese shoji, the screen contains a direct reference to the grid motif used extensively by Daniel Hechter. As with the Yves Saint Laurent area, the designers have separated showrooms from design studios and administrative areas. Glass walls within the showrooms create private sales areas.

The entry to the Daniel Hechter
space features a shoji-inspired
screening device behind the
stone-topped reception desk.
The palette combines wood and
stone in a range of neutral tones.

The entry to the YSL space
progresses through a cat-walk-like
corridor into a reception area
that features an elegantly minimal
composition of black and
white stone.

The reception area of the Daniel Hechter showroom incorporates the subtle sophistication of the clothing line, with a muted palette and simple geometric lines.

The unusual desk of the reception area complements the linearity of the YSL logo. Dropped, sculptured ceiling soffits establish the theme of different visual dimensions used to provide privacy for visiting buyers in the individual showrooms.

The preliminary floorplans.

The layered screening walls in the Daniel Hechter space feature a grid borrowed from the corporate logo. In addition to designating the boundaries of the individual interior showrooms, they also add visual interest to the neutral environment.

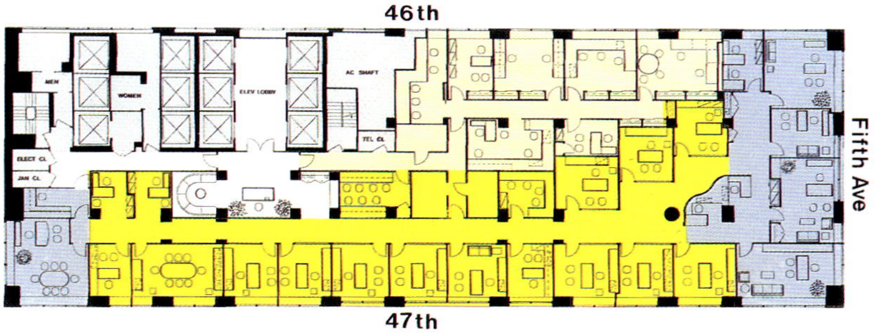


46th
Fifth Ave
47th


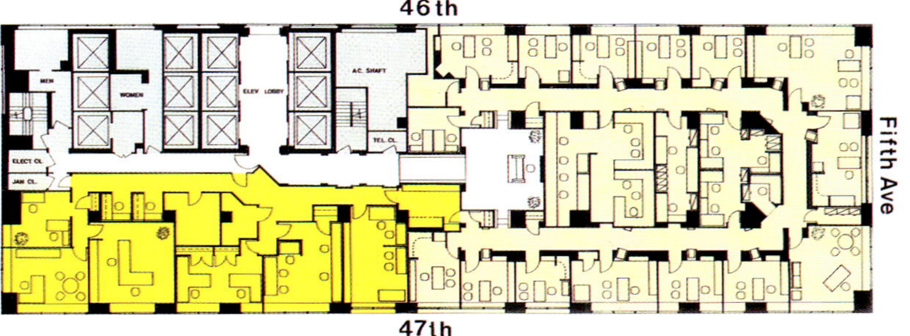


46th
Fifth Ave
47th

# Integrated
# Resources, Inc.
## New York, New York 1989

# Integrated Resources, Inc., a financial services firm, commissioned The

Switzer Group, Inc. to design its work space on four floors at Zeckendorf Towers, 10 Union Square East. Working on a fast-track schedule that allowed personnel relocation to begin one year from the inception of the project, the design team completed a 450,000-square-foot facility supporting the activities of 1,300 employees. Ongoing reorganization and the tight schedule demanded adjustments in the field. The necessary versatility was provided by systems furniture workstations and by the use of raised flooring to provide power to the offices. The installation included an expansive atrium/lobby, a brokerage/trading facility, a 20,000-square-foot data center, cafeteria, lounge, multi-purpose conference rooms, medical center and fitness center. The Switzer Group, Inc. also designed its off-site Data Center supporting National Facilities. The Union Square project was the culmination of designs The Switzer Group, Inc. had executed for Integrated Resources, Inc., including at 666 3rd Ave. (two floors), 733 3rd Ave. (8 floors), and other space at 800 2nd Avenue.

Each floor faced the preexisting atrium, which the designers retrofitted as the dining area. All employee offices were arranged to overlook the atrium, which the designers landscaped with trees and a central fountain. The program dictated private offices for executives and management levels, an executive boardroom, secretarial workstations and support spaces, including a full-service kitchen and servery, data and telecommunications facilities, and a mail room. Private elevators at the ground floor provided entrance for employees and visitors only. Central reception and administrative offices, along with human resources, medical and fitness facilities occupied the second floor.

The designers used an open plan for the majority of the workspace, and installed one of the city's first completely raised flooring systems to supply communications, power and data needs of the client. The open plan maximized the flow of natural light through the interior. Fully demountable workstations allowed for considerable flexibility and adaptability, including, when necessary, moving into private offices. Modulations varied the ceiling and floor planes, establishing traffic patterns and providing visual interest. Ductwork and ceilings could be reconfigured as well, allowing for the possibility of a universal facility.

The executive area of Integrated Resources, Inc.

The expansive lobby opens off the entry corridor.

Arched corridor and
reception desk.

The executive boardroom.

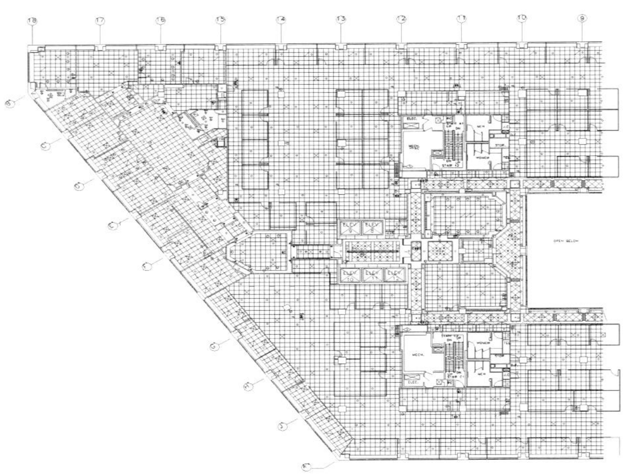

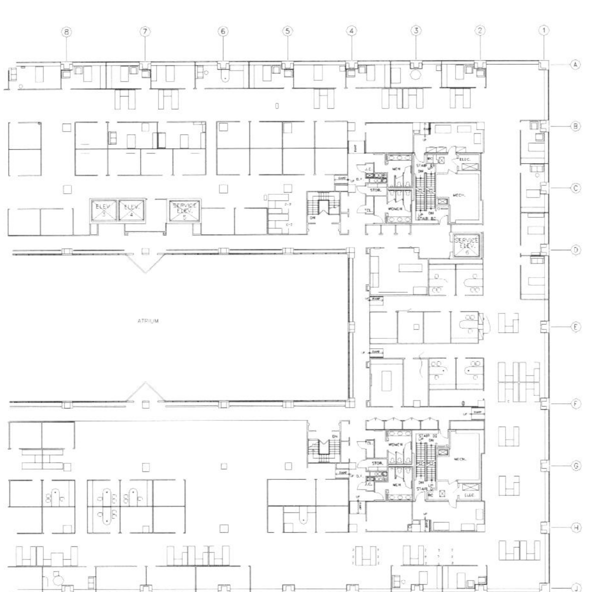

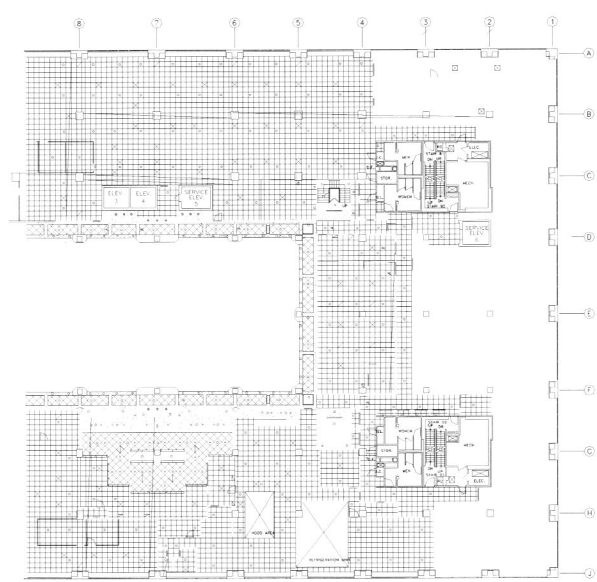

Reflected ceiling plans reveal the planning logic exercised to organize the client's continuously growing operation.

Schematic drawing
of interior circulation
overlooking
the atrium space.

The designers retrofit the existing atrium to accommodate a dining facility.

Schematic drawing of an active atrium space.

Design as an
Understanding
of the Business
Environment:

# EMI Music Worldwide
## New York, New York 1991

The 27,000-square-foot New York headquarters for EMI Music Worldwide occupies three floors of Carnegie Hall Tower in midtown Manhattan. The client wanted contemporary interiors to reflect its popular music product and executive offices that would serve the multiple purposes of its executives. To address these needs, the designers developed a state-of-the-art facility equipped with sound systems throughout as well as built-in sound systems for each private office.

A grand, central stairway, the primary design focus, provides internal circulation through the three floors of offices. The second level contains the reception area, which features a luminous ceiling and a custom concrete and metal reception desk. The terrazzo floor of the entry area extends through to the central stairwell, drawing the visitor's attention to the stair; terrazzo lines the entire three-floor stairwell, framing a custom stair with custom millwork and terrazzo risers. The lower level houses support areas, including service areas, the pantry and the mailroom.

A wall finished with a custom paint treatment rises at the top of the stairwell; this architectural gesture fans out into the upper floor, which contains executive and presentation facilities. The executive offices, designed for small private meetings, occupy the rear of the floor with the support staff at the front. The chairman's office is on a grand scale, suited to his more elaborate entertaining needs, with Italian marble flooring and doors that open onto a terrace. The presentation room exists behind massive metal doors that can be closed to provide sound barriers or opened to offer views of midtown Manhattan and a flow of natural daylight. A retractable screen lowers from the ceiling for visual presentations.

EMI

The terrazzo floors and curving lines of the entrance lobby create visual links to the custom terrazzo stairway.

Conference room with articulated ceiling plane composed of dropped soffits and both direct and indirect lighting.

Schematic drawing of conference room.

Internal hallway with curved wall and enlivened ceiling plane.

The spacious executive office features a sculptured ceiling and natural light.

Schematic drawing of executive office.

The primary design focus of this building, the horseshoe-shaped stair featuring terrazzo risers and custom millwork connects the three levels of EMI.

Reception area with brushed aluminum reception desk.

The executive floor plan.

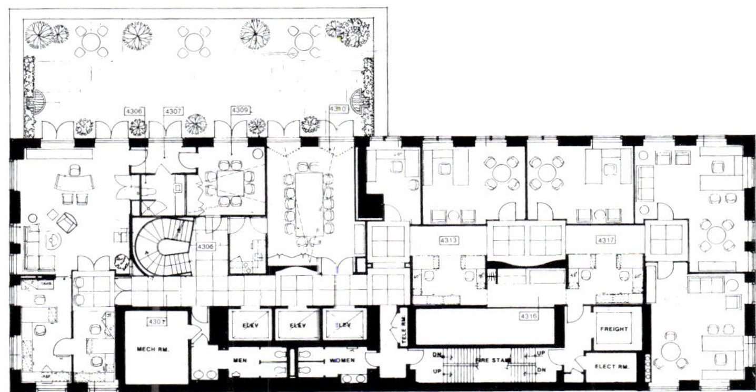

Design as an
Understanding
of the Business
Environment:

# New Charleston Capital Management
## New York, New York 1992

New Charleston Capital Management, a private investment firm
with southern roots, established its corporate headquarters in the penthouse of 135 East 57th Street and
commissioned The Switzer Group, Inc. to design them. Both client and designers decided to appoint the
space with the traditional details and transitional elements that recall the heritage of the firm's partners
and convey the requisite sense of responsibility, comfort and fiduciary responsibility to the clientele.
Georgian elements and details of the interior architecture were lavishly applied in order to establish the
character that distinguishes New Charleston Capital Management among its peers in the financial world.

The 7,000-square-foot facility included 15 private offices for the investment bankers arrayed along
the floor's periphery, as well as executive office space, workstations for support staff and conference
facilities. The client requested a rather classic, Georgian-inspired decor to connect this executive headquarters with the firm's southern origins. The oval-shaped reception area provided an elegant entry
graced with precious detail. Initially conceived as a jewel-box-like space, the reception area was appointed
with antiques, including the desk flanked by pairs of chairs. The carpet was custom designed to replicate
the ornamental pattern of marble flooring in the entry hall of Charleston's historic homes; other applied
details include custom period-style moldings for walls and ceiling.

Antique and reproduction furniture was used throughout to establish a sense of tradition and
the continuity of history. Handcrafted mahogany paneling, custom woven carpets and lavish fabrics were
commissioned to reinforce the desired aura of history and tradition. The boardroom includes a massive
mahogany conference table, elaborate draperies hanging at the windows and a pendant-shaped
crystal chandelier.

Special areas include a professional kitchen fitted with a custom exhaust for the ovens and a
full-service executive dining room for entertaining clients.

The elevator lobby and reception incorporate traditional design details to establish a sense of the firm's Southern heritage.

The oval-shaped reception area includes an elliptical desk, a dramatically articulated oval ceiling and a custom carpet.

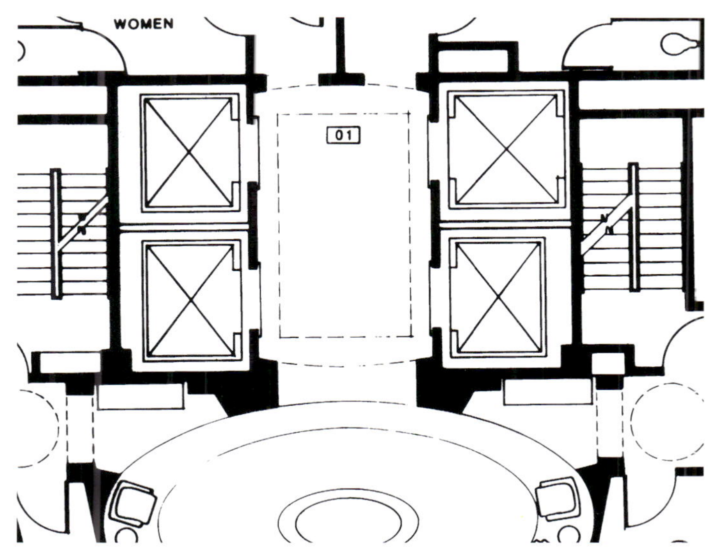





The secretarial support room is characterized by a column and coffered ceiling.

The preliminary schematic drawing of the secretarial support room.

Plan for the elevator lobby and reception area reveals the designers' sense of geometric logic.

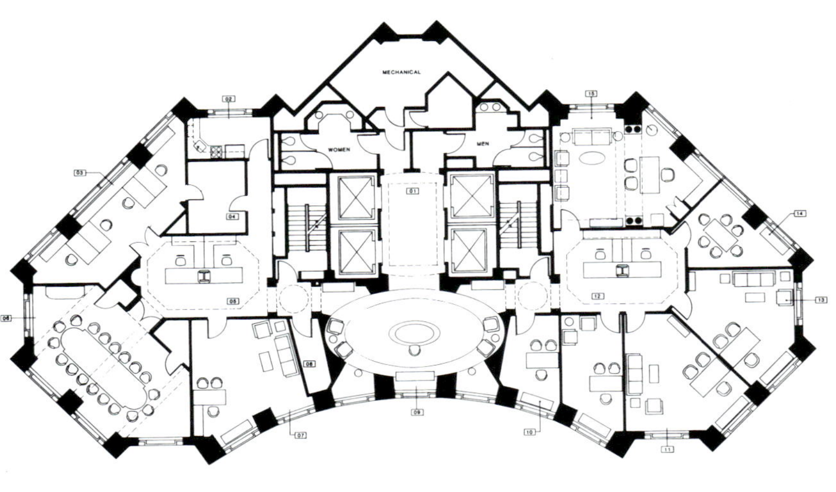


MECHANICAL
WOMEN
MEN

Partner's office with traditional furniture, fabrics and drapery treatments.

Executive office with Queen Ann-style furniture and paneled walls.

The plan for the entire floor.

The boardroom includes the same level of detail, with coffered ceiling and pendant fixtures, traditional ornamental window treatments and art.

# Chase Manhattan Bank, MetroTech Center Corporate Dining, Training and Central Services Facility Brooklyn, New York 1992

When Chase Manhattan Bank decided to relocate its operations group
to 1.7 million square feet of space in Brooklyn's MetroTech Center, it commissioned The Switzer Group, Inc.
to design the ancillary spaces. The program included 350,000 square feet on several floors of the overall
complex, divided into two distinct projects: the training center and the corporate dining and central services
facility. Integrated into the design were such specialized systems as conveyors, exhaust systems and
food service systems. Among the many challenges was the need to design each floor, some as large as
90,000-square-feet, in such a way as to create the illusion of a smaller, more comprehensible space.

The training center consists of more than 30 multi-use areas such as conference rooms, training
rooms and classrooms, A/V support services, an A/V broadcast room, furniture storage rooms and the
training center's administration offices. The center, like the entire complex, was built on a raised flooring
system that provides for the easy access and flexibility necessary to meet the technological demands
of teleconferencing, computer communications and satellite broadcasting.

The corporate dining and central services facility is comprised of corporate dining rooms, a staff
restaurant, officer dining rooms, lounges, security, reprographics, mail processing, central supply, a
fitness center, a medical center and an employee services center. The 1,400-seat cafeteria is defined
by communal spaces that break out into more intimate dining areas. The executive dining area seats
75 to100 people, with private rooms and maitre d' service. Among the other areas included in the
program were computer printing, bulk storage, shipping and receiving, engineering operations and
messenger functions.

The entrance to the training area.

Schematic drawing
of entrance.

The 1,400-seat cafeteria opens with an expansive, tiled food-service area that opens up into a series of communal spaces.

Schematic drawing
of restaurant entry.

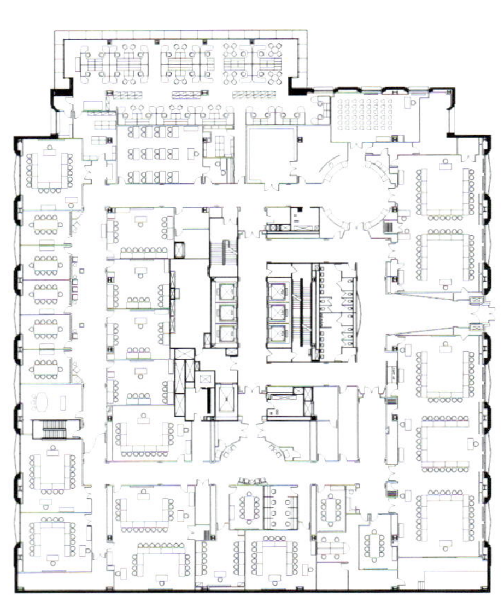

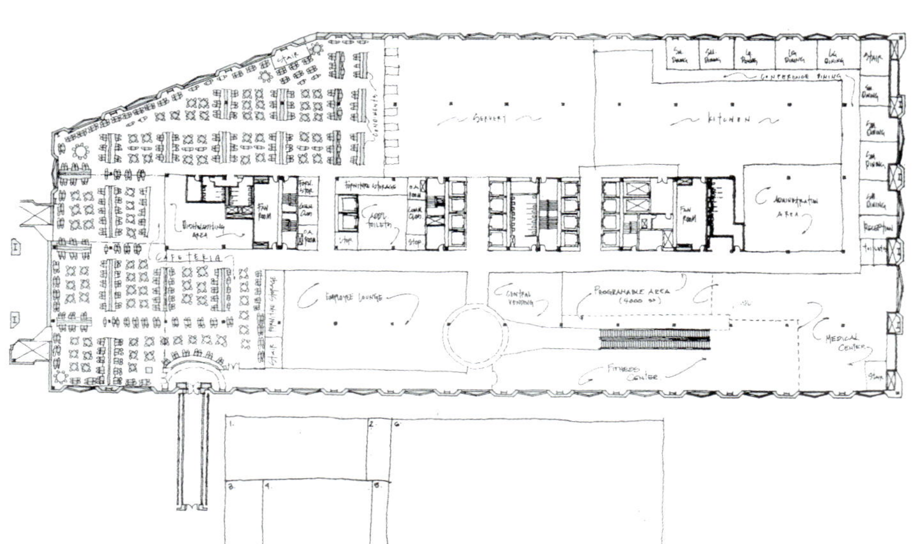

The training support facility includes open-plan areas for staff.

The communal areas of the cafeteria break out in to more intimate spaces.

The floorplan to the conference training center.

Preliminary studies of the cafeteria.

Models of final plans.

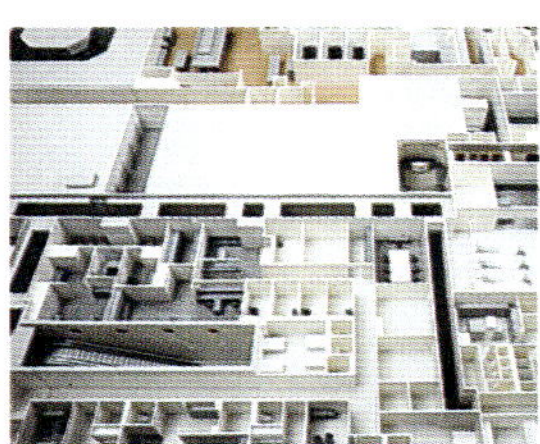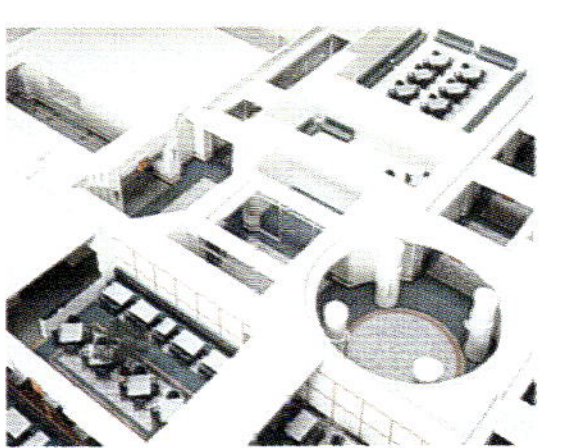

Design as an Understanding of the Business Environment:

# Consolidated Edison Company of New York, Inc.

## Con Ed "Learning Center" Educational and Training Facility, Long Island City, New York 1993

# Consolidated Edison Company of New York, Inc.

commissioned The Switzer Group, Inc. to manage, plan and design a new education training center on nine acres along the East River in Long Island City. The project required converting and retrofitting the site's two existing structures into one building that would include training areas duplicating actual locations and "real-life" situations, incorporate imaginative teaching aids and provide easy access to equipment. Con Ed needed teaching environments that simulated everything from outdoor underground service and cabling to exteriors and interiors of private homes, as well as a fossil fuel plant control center.

The old buildings were gutted completely. The remaining skeletal structure established the parameters of the new plan. A new, 400-foot-long façade consisted of a simple composition of pre-cast concrete and brick punctuated by a series of openings punched for the strategic entry of daylight through the building face. New air-conditioning, heating, electrical systems, windows and roof incorporated a wide range of energy conservation techniques. The fast-track schedule set a 12-month time frame to complete the project from design through demolition, construction and move-in.

The configuration of the new building opens up from a central lobby. A skylighted arcade serves as the building's spine, containing the primary circulation elements and providing a great influx of natural light. The lobby and arcade connect the buildings at different points, forming break-out areas adjacent to the meeting space, dining room and class rooms. The more public areas and the cafeteria are housed at ground level, with the upper levels divided into labs, workshops and office spaces. The third floor and mechanical level were set back, establishing a strong north/south axis and emphasizing the building entrance.

As completed, the Learning Center includes a flexible meeting space for as many as 1,200 people and offices for the core staff of trainers and librarians. Among its other features are a full-service cafeteria with a dining room that opens to an outdoor terrace facing the East River and the Manhattan skyline and a complete reference library with study space and information exchange areas where students meet informally on the way to class. The Queens Chamber of Commerce and the American Institute of Architects recognized the project in 1994 for Excellence in Design.

The architects employed state-of-the-art technology to simulate "real-life" scenarios in each of these classrooms in the training facility.

CHECK ALIVE
BOTH SIDES
Con Edison

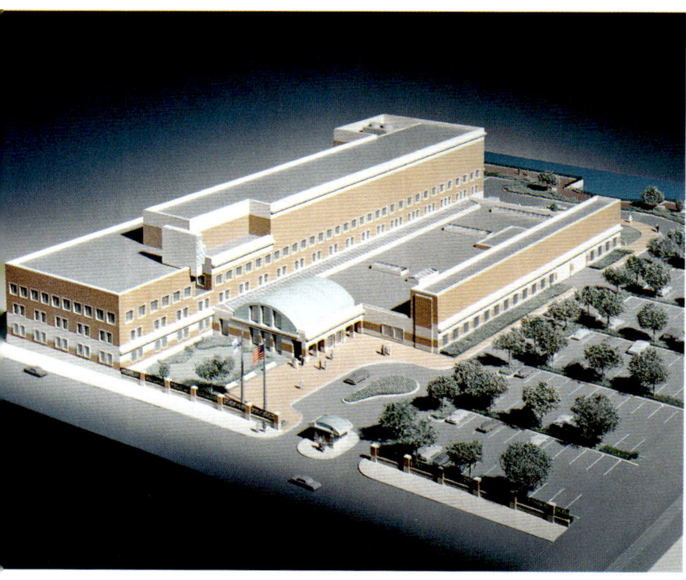

This classroom replicates the basement of a house, part of Con Edison's innovative training program.

This classroom includes a replica of a truck for emergency set-up and instrument training purposes.

The scale model provides an overview of the entire facility.

Presentation drawing of renovated facility with parking.

The cafeteria and servery
include an etched
glass wall and tiled surfaces
that add interest
and sparkle to the room.

The cafeteria boasts windows with views of the 59th Street bridge, and skylights
with special sun deflection features.

The auditorium was designed with special acoustic and lighting treatments.

Design as an
Understanding
of the Business
Environment:

# IBM, Regional Headquarters
## Cranford, New Jersey 1993

When IBM designated its New Jersey regional headquarters as a test site for alternative
ways of doing business based on the concept of "free address" design, the company consolidated its
four New Jersey offices—1,200 employees and 400,000 square feet—into a 100,000-square-foot facility
with a goal of four employees per workstation. Mobile employees primarily work outside the office with a
car, a laptop computer and a cell phone, using the regional headquarters facility as a home base.
The employees present an identification card at an employee reception area. The card is entered into a
computer that assigns the employee to a workstation and automatically transfers telephone lines for the
day. After the initial occupancy, IBM surpassed its goal, utilizing the facility at a ratio of eight employees
per workstation.

Entry is divided: customers at the front, employees at the rear. A central aisle, dubbed "main
street," divides the floor into a simple hierarchy. Permanent occupants surround the vice president on one
side. Mobile staff occupies the other side of the aisle. Employees' portable files are stored in a central-
aisle filing system. The vice president can stand and view all employees in residence, given workstations
with 6-foot by 8-foot by 4-foot-high dimensions.

Two-thirds of the total space houses workstations; the remaining third contains ancillary facilities
and amenities, such as reception, customer service area, special training rooms and two types of conference spaces. General sales meetings are held on the open floor with a microphone system. Amenities also
include a computer room, full-service cafeteria with kitchen and food warming capabilities for 200
people, mail room, restrooms and reproduction area. Customer service occupies the front of the facility.

Acoustical panels inserted 6 inches below the ceiling deck and the white noise of the air conditioning
help absorb sound. To achieve an ambient glow, lights were mounted on support beams. Pendant lights
also hang along the corridors. Heating is based on a standard placement 10 feet within the perimeter.
The air-conditioning system divides the open space into three zones. LAN (local area network) closets were
installed to supply connectivity to the workstations. The concrete floor was replaced to lay power lines
beneath walkways and connect them with desks. Raised floor tiles conceal the electrical cables in
the 10,000-square-foot computer room. This project received recognition from *Interior Design*, *National
Officing* (a Japanese publication), *Business Week*, *The New York Times*, and *Facilities Design and
Management*.

Four-foot high dividing walls partially enclose each 60-square-foot
work area, which includes a desk with basic office supplies, connections
for telephone, data port, LAN and host and remote printing.

The interior features a hive of shared desks, assigned according to the needs of visiting
employees; portable files are stored in a central aisle filing system.

An early rendering of
the proposed interior space.

The exterior of the building exhibits the well-lit, glass-encased entryway.

This computer rendering displays a cross-section of the building.

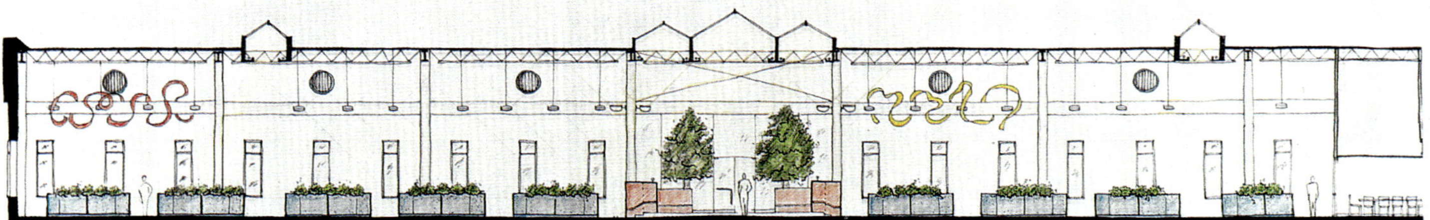

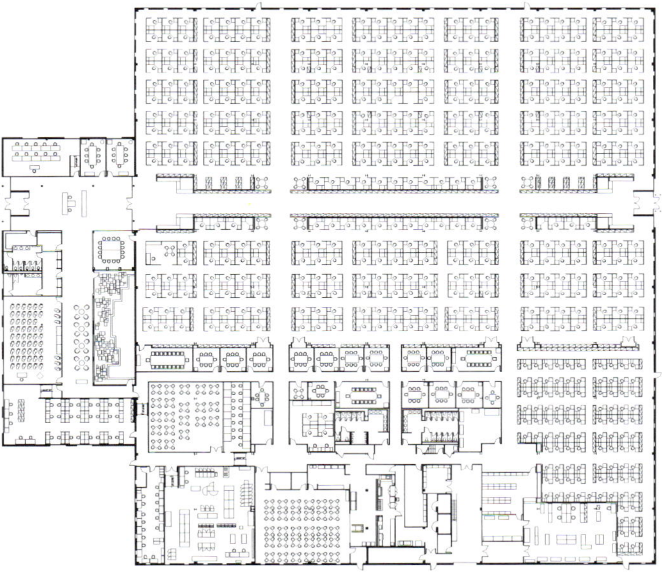

A central check-in point directs visitors, mobile employees and resident staff as necessary.

The floor plan reveals
the spatial economy of the
hoteling option.

# Design as an Understanding of the Business Environment:

# Westinghouse Broadcasting
## New York, New York 1995

# When Westinghouse Broadcasting relocated to 42,000 square feet

at 200 Park Avenue from its former headquarters at 888 Seventh Avenue, it commissioned The Switzer Group, Inc. to create comfortable, presentable spaces for meeting with clients in the entertainment industry. The design brief was to provide the highest quality within a transitional style, and the latest in technology that is easily accessible but not readily apparent. The space's inherent problems included low ceiling heights, and an enormous building core with extremely long corridors.

Because this location housed executives almost exclusively, along with some sales department personnel and support staff, the environment desired was living room-like to encourage informal, personal contact with clients. The plan does, however, adhere to a more or less traditional hierarchical organization, with higher level executives placed closer to the president. Circulation organizes the internal space around the core. Three sizes of offices accommodate the secretaries, executives and president.

The reconfigured floor now includes state-of-the-art conference rooms with teleconferencing capabilities, executive boardrooms and a cafeteria. Secretarial stations are custom designed in wood. The reception desk combines green marble with figured anigre. The board room features a sophisticated audio-visual wall with synchronized lighting, front projection and television monitors for the display of programs from all of Westinghouse's station affiliates. The Switzer Group, Inc. also served as the client's art consultant for the interior, choosing antiques—such as 18th-century Japanese screens—and more contemporary works, including paintings by Robert Rauschenberg and other celebrated contemporary artists.

The many windows of the executive office provide natural light.

Corridor detail.

The elevator lobby displays glass entrance doors and the polished marble floors that run throughout the building.

Marble reception desk and main corridor.

GROUP
W

The executive boardroom includes a sophisticated audio-visual wall with synchronized lighting, front projection and television monitors for displaying the programs of all Westinghouse affiliate stations.

The main reception area is accented by an antique Oriental screen.

Not withstanding the low ceilings and difficult fenestration details, the design maximizes the stunning views of the New York City skyline.

# Design as an Understanding of the Business Environment:

# Citibank, NA Flagship Model Branch
## New York, New York, 1991

When Citibank, NA decided to reorient its retail operations to automated banking, to promote the ATM machine and increase its use by making it more user friendly, it commissioned The Switzer Group, Inc. to redesign its 20,000-square-foot flagship model branch at 399 Park Avenue. The project was conceived as a prototype— the "branch of the future"-for future implementation at Citibank sites throughout the tri-state area. The Switzer Group, Inc. team was the first to translate Citibank's new standards from an image branding industrial design package to an architectural "kit-of-parts," making it flexible enough to adapt easily to the specific conditions of the individual branch locations.

The problem for The Switzer Group, Inc. team was to make the package coherent: the designers had to understand all the pieces and parts in order to take all the individual standards— marketing, displays, furniture, panels, plastic laminates, ceilings and lighting-and lay the elements out in a way that customers could best experience the Citibank approach to banking. The first point of customer reference was a meeter/greeter desk. Next in the progression was the ATM platform area, where a wide variety of banking services take place, including the dispensing of money. The rear of the bank was reserved for more private transactions. The design team also addressed security issues with great care.

This Park Avenue branch was the first of many easily recognizable banking icons implemented throughout Citibank's network of facilities.

The entrance to the ATM space is well lit and secure.

The ATM platform area was given a staggered, setback design to ensure customer privacy.

The teller line.

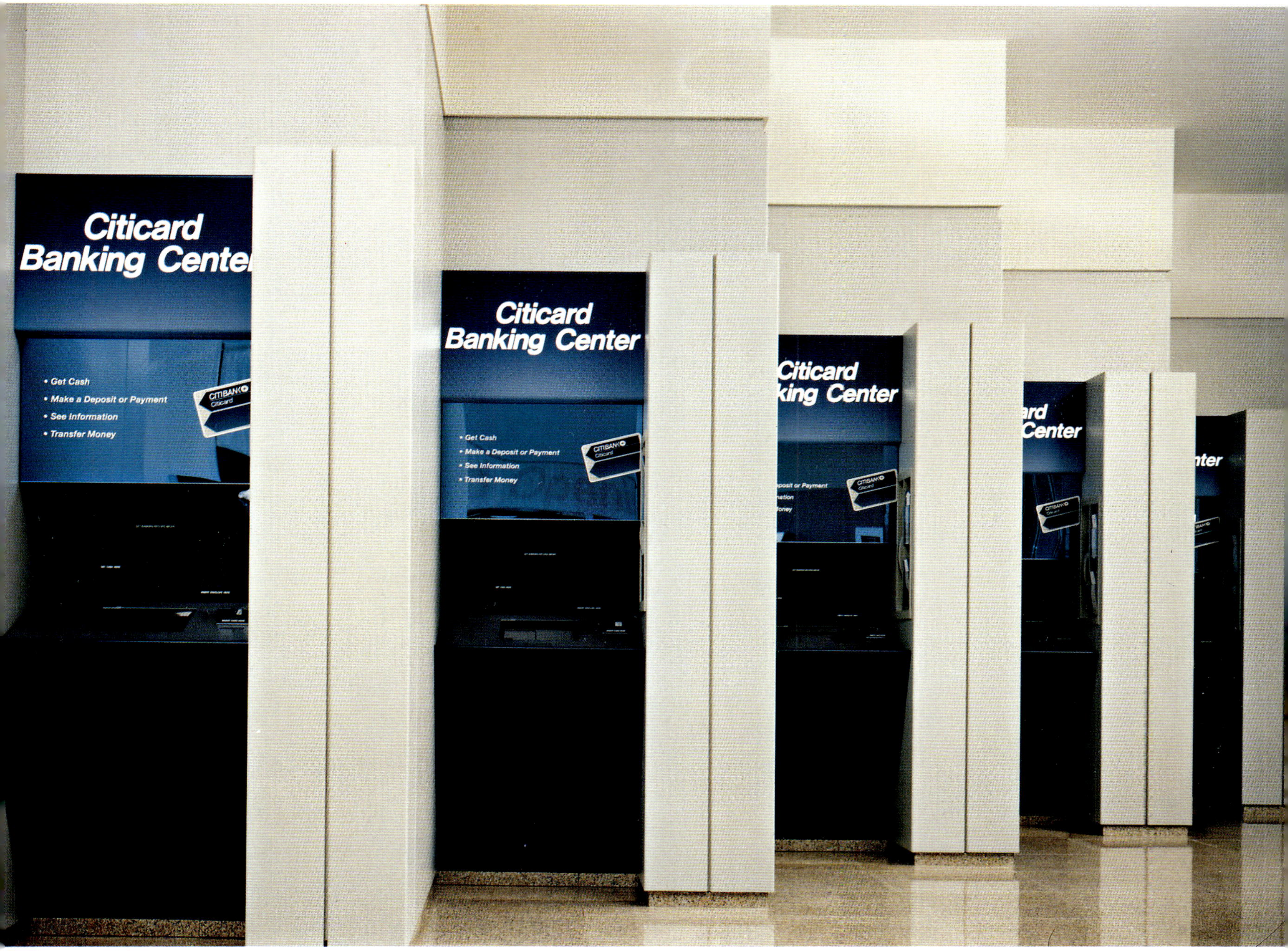

Citicard
Banking Center
• Get Cash
• Make a Deposit or Payment
• See Information
• Transfer Money
CITIBANK
Citicard
Citicard
Banking Center
• Get Cash
• Make a Deposit or Payment
• See Information
• Transfer Money


CITIBANK

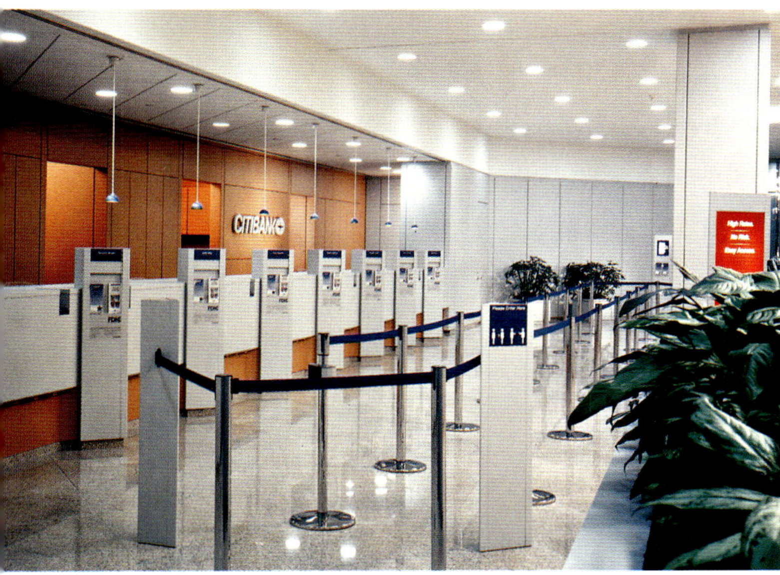

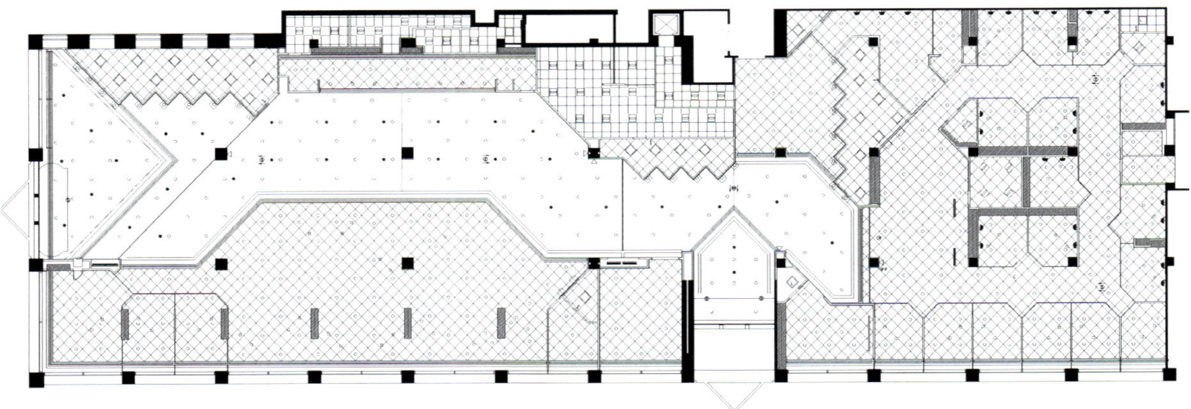

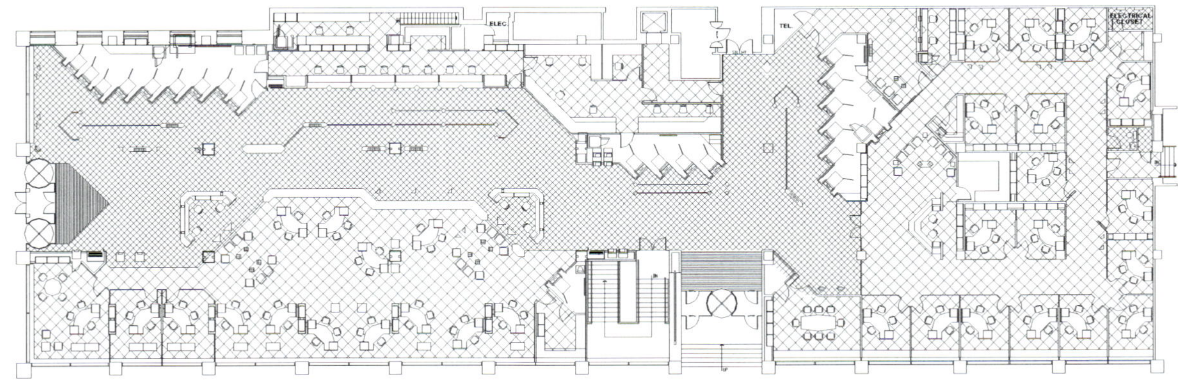

Welcome to Citibank

Floor plans for upper and lower levels.

An area for more private transactions occupies the rear of the floor.

Meeter/greeter
desk.

The teller
service area.

Customer service and loan offices.

The waiting area is located near the glass-encased offices.

Design as an Understanding of the Business Environment:

# Design as an Understanding of the Business Environment:

# The Equitable, 1290 Avenue of the Americas

## New York, New York 1997

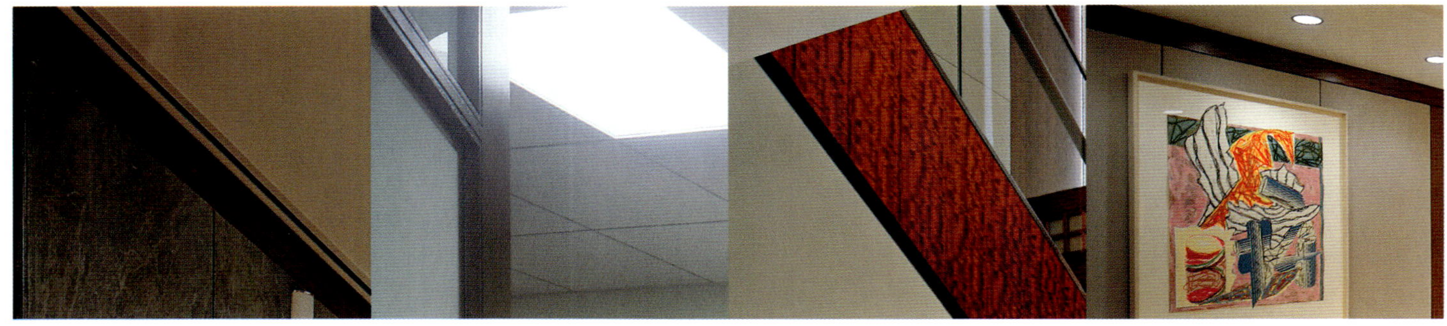

In its new headquarters, The Equitable wanted to reduce its overall square footage from 1,000,000 to 550,000. To accomplish the desired consolidation, the designers developed a layout that consisted of 30 percent closed office space and 70 percent open plan. The configuration was dictated by a series of structural setbacks in the building's perimeter. The Switzer Group, Inc. utilized an innovative "top down" master planning process to effectively and realistically achieve such a dramatic reduction in occupancy cost and square footage.

The floor plan was organized to make the most efficient use of space, with primary circulation occurring around the core and also around the perimeter. One end of each floor terminates in a conference room with two offices. Other factors influencing the floor plan included the flow of natural light and the relationship between worker and window. The client wanted a lot of ambient light, a preference that affected the modularity of the furniture. Glass paneling was incorporated into the systems furniture to increase the flow of daylight into the core. Floors 9 through 16 are long and narrow; the 17th floor is the beginning of a tower. The 16th floor serves as the executive core; the 15th includes the cafeteria, training and conference facilities. The facility also includes a data center, themed cafe, law offices and library, mail and archives facility, boardroom, computer labs and multiple teleconference areas.

Departments were allowed to personalize their areas from a menu of three colors for interior-exterior workstation panels, as well as a choice of workstations and chairs. Two levels of workstations with 11 possible configurations were ultimately developed for the managerial and technical staff, which numbers 1,000: a 72-square-foot E-level workstation and a 100-square-foot D-level station. The E-level version included the option of movable partitions that can be raised or lowered for privacy, a special feature used only in the legal department. The larger D-level workstations were used as a transition for the 354 employees who were transferring to open plan offices, including mid-level management, senior level technical staff and senior level human resources people. Two closed office plans, differentiated only by the exclusion or inclusion of private closet space, were developed for the professional level employees.

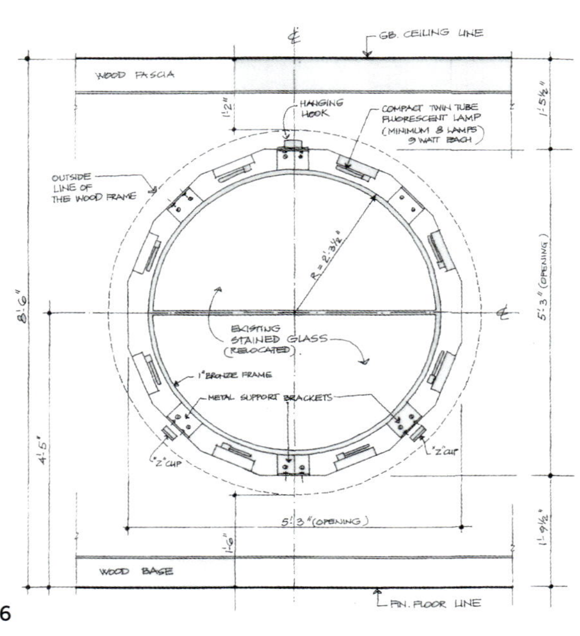

GB. CEILING LINE
WOOD FASCIA
HANGING HOOK
COMPACT TWIN TUBE FLUORESCENT LAMP (MINIMUM 8 LAMPS) 9 WATT EACH
OUTSIDE LINE OF THE WOOD FRAME
R = 2'-3½"
EXISTING STAINED GLASS (RELOCATED)
1" BRONZE FRAME
METAL SUPPORT BRACKETS
"2" CLIP
"2" CLIP
5'-3" (OPENING)
5'-3" (OPENING)
WOOD BASE
FIN. FLOOR LINE
1'-2"
1'-5½"
8'-6"
4'-5"
1'-0"
1'-9½"

WHITE GB. CLG. W/ DOWNLIGHT.
BRASS TUBE PICTURE LIGHT
OLD LANDSCAPE PAINTING.
DON'T SHOW PAINTING HERE
WOOD FRAME
FABRIC
FABRIC
VIEW TO THE CONFERENCE RM.
WOOD DOOR W/ BEVELED GLASS PANELS
OVAL MIRROR IN WOOD (CONFEDERATE) FRAME
CHINESE VASE CLOISONNE
CONSOLE CREDENZA
WOOD DOOR WITH BEVELED GLASS PANELS AND BRASS HANDLE.
OVAL TABLE W/ BRASS LEGS.
STONE SHELF IN THE NICHE
CARPET
CARPET STRIPS
CARPET BORDER
WOOD BASE.
ANTE ROOM

The executive elevator lobby features a leaded glass window.

The view looking down the executive corridor.

Detail of the leaded
glass window, a symbol
that has stayed with
The Equitable from its
first building.

Plans for the executive
waiting room.

Rendering of the executive and administrative floors connected by an interior stair.

Detail of interior stair connecting the 15th and 16th floors.

Rendering illustrating a treatment of elevator lobby with connecting stair.

A breakout area on the 15th floor exemplifies the transitional
style of the interior.

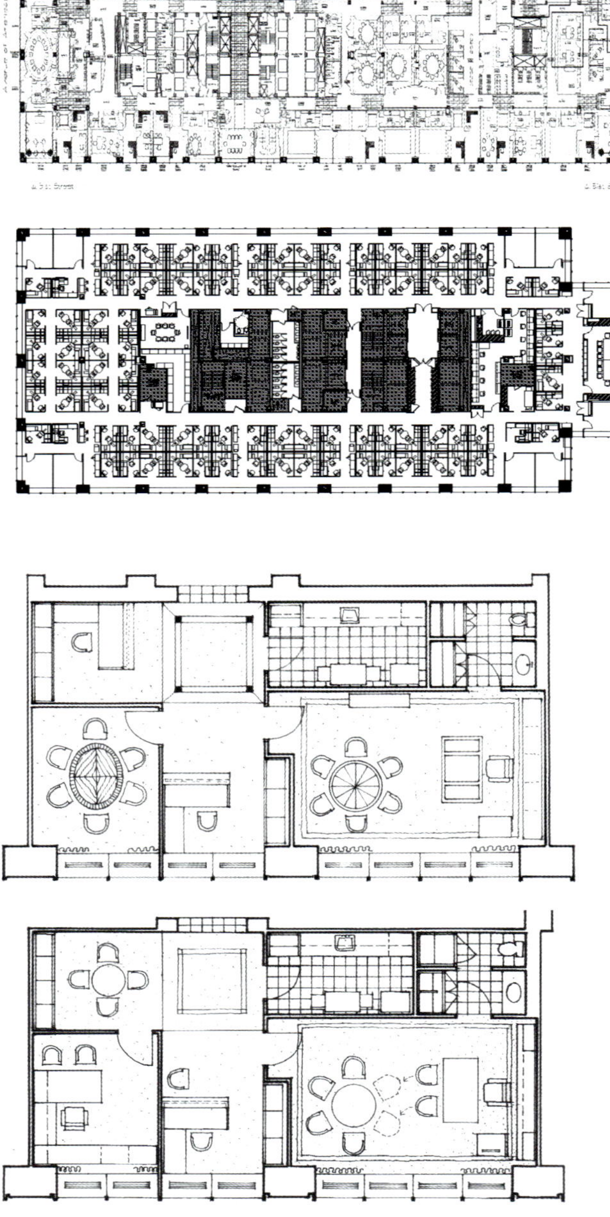

Plans for the upper tower floors.

Clockwise from top left: training center waiting room; typical conference room; cafeteria; legal department library.

# Forstmann
# & Company
## New York, New York 1999

When Forstmann & Company, a 186-year-old manufacturer and whole-
sale distributor of wool and wool-blend fabrics, relocated to a 15,000-square-foot space on Seventh
Avenue, it commissioned The Switzer Group, Inc. to turn-key design and construct an interior that encom-
passed closed offices, viewing rooms for visiting buyers, a central open office area with workstations,
pantry, mail/copy room, a materials library, a studio for the development of patterns and prints for new
product lines and storage areas for materials and products. The new space incorporates high ceilings and
exposed structural elements to create a sense of openness and volume. The main focus of the decor
consists of galvanized air ducts, large reflector downlights, sprinkler piping and the metal troughs that
contain cable and wires for the office's communications and computer systems.

Private offices, extending along the space's long, windowed perimeters, are shaped by rolling
metal-and-glass partial-height walls that slide into open and closed positions along a grid of tracks at
the floor. The lower portion of the walls is backpainted glass; the upper, clear. A ceiling soffit reiterates
the grid of the interior plan. The system of rolling/sliding walls permits greater accessibility and more
efficient use of the interior office space since no clearances for door swings were necessary. It also allows
the offices to blend visually into the rest of the interior.

The color scheme tends to warm earth tones with accents of the slate floor in the reception area
and custom millwork elements in the showroom spaces. The lighting plan combines down and ambient
fixtures. Most of the client's existing furniture was reused for the new interior.

FORSTMANN

Reception area.

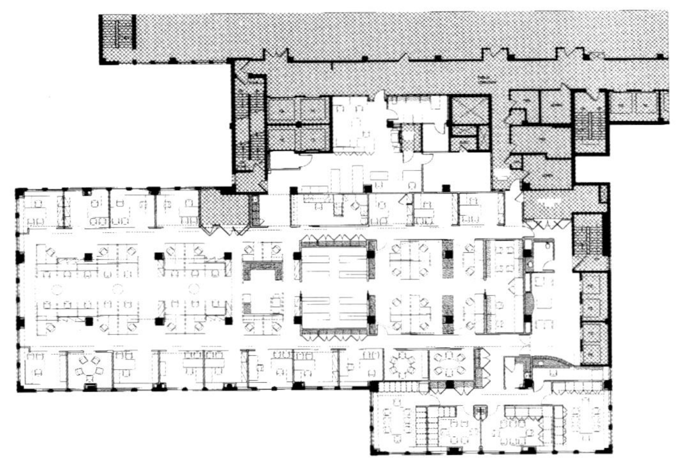

Detail of furniture layout plan.

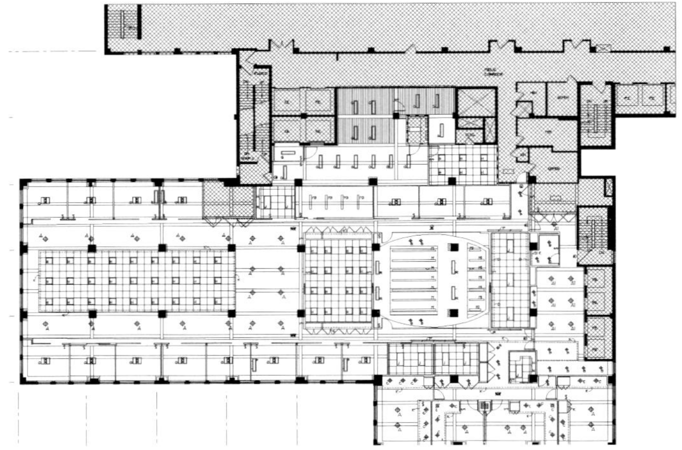

Detail of reflected ceiling plan.

High ceilings with exposed
ductwork, large reflector downlights,
sprinkler piping and metal
cable troughs provide considerable
visual interest to the interior.

Design as an
Understanding
of the Business
Environment:

# Allen & Overy
## New York, New York 1998

# Allen & Overy,

**Allen & Overy,** a London-based law firm with offices in 19 countries, commissioned The Switzer Group, Inc. to redesign its New York offices to provide an optimum working environment. Asked initially to modify the existing Rockefeller Center space, The Switzer Group, Inc. ultimately renovated the entire interior in order to accommodate the required number of employees and prepare for projected growth. The program for the New York office included the elevator lobby, reception area, conference room, executive conference room, war room, copy/fax room, data, private offices, workstations, a library, pantry and a copy room.

The overall look is clean and traditional, but the use of lighter woods combined with custom details provides a contemporary twist. Key features include the use of anigre for the reception desk and workstation details. Private offices extend along the perimeter of the interior. A glass panel above the inner wall of each partner's office allows for the flow of natural light into the core.

Lawyers, paralegals and administrative staff occupy workstations directly across the circulation aisle from the partners' offices in order to achieve easy communication among personnel. A large, glass-walled conference room overlooking the Rockefeller Center Promenade opens directly off the reception area. The executive conference room divides easily into two smaller spaces when necessity demands, and includes state-of-the-art audiovisual equipment that can be upgraded with new technology. A smaller-than-usual law library is located opposite the executive conference area: instead of keeping traditional hard copy versions of legal journals and reference books, the firm uses on-line resources extensively, allowing the designers to allocate more space for other areas.

An unusual aspect of this project was the process itself. The Switzer Group, Inc. worked directly with the project management team in the client's London office: all team members were in contact daily; e-mail was used extensively for project communications, including drawing review. While Allen & Overy did allow the New York Partners to participate in design selections, all critical decisions were made between the London office and The Switzer Group, Inc. staff in New York.

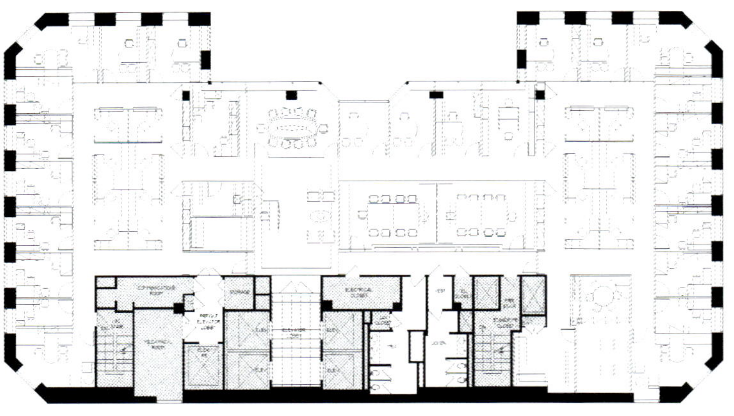

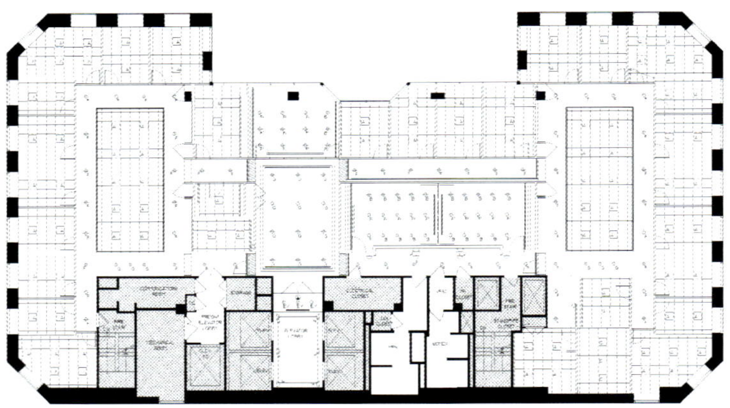

The reception area features a custom-designed desk made from the blond wood used throughout the interior. The adjacent conference room overlooks Rockefeller Center.

Lawyers, paralegals and administrative staff are located directly across from partners' offices; fabric-covered work station panels and anigre wood surfaces and trim provide a degree of elegance to the open office.

Detail of
furniture layout.

Detail of
reflected ceiling plan.

The conference room accommodates 12, and is fully equipped for audiovisual requirements.

Private partners' offices are arrayed along the perimeter.

# Chase Manhattan Bank, Securities Lending Facility

**New York, New York** 1998

The Switzer Group. Inc, designed and renovated a 35,000-square-foot floor
at Four New York Plaza to house the securities management and trading facilities for Chase-Manhattan
Bank. The base building's existing infrastructure was inadequate to support the client's electrical, communications and data requirements. As part of the conversion, the entire floor was raised to house wiring
underneath. The building has a side core, with only the north side remaining open, which meant the
designers had to establish an inner core to accommodate such functional amenities as restrooms.

Security issues were also pressing. Entry is available only through a private, wood-paneled reception area. A glass-walled ramp behind the main desk provides access to the main floor. A glass wall
exposes the 5,000-square-foot trading room to visiting customers without disturbing the trading staff.
The designers also provided an opening in the trading room's glass wall through which to pass tickets.

Like the other building occupants, Chase Manhattan initially had an east-west orientation. The
Switzer Group, Inc. reconfigured the space along a north-south axis in order to maximize available square
footage, creating a new standard for other floors in the building. Private offices rim the entire area. The
central volume is filled with an open plan system. The traditional hierarchy was maintained by locating
supervisors on the east and west ends of the floor.

Chase Manhattan typically approaches its interior design program by incorporating standardized
workstations. In this facility, three standards of workstations were implemented. In order to maximize the
amount of natural light flowing into the center from the perimeter, workstations were set at different
heights. The space was also broken up with fabric and glass panels. In addition, the designers modified
the space so that larger and smaller workstations were configured together.

This particular facility features three executive conference rooms. Other conference rooms are
occupied primarily by support staff and used for multimedia presentations. Wood conference tables
incorporate state-of-the-art technology. Computers can be connected at the table and displayed on a
wall-inset video monitor. Wood paneling in the reception and conference rooms complements the
Chase Manhattan standards.

The reception area features wood paneling and an articulated ceiling plane.

A glass-walled ramp behind the reception desk provides access to the main trading floor.

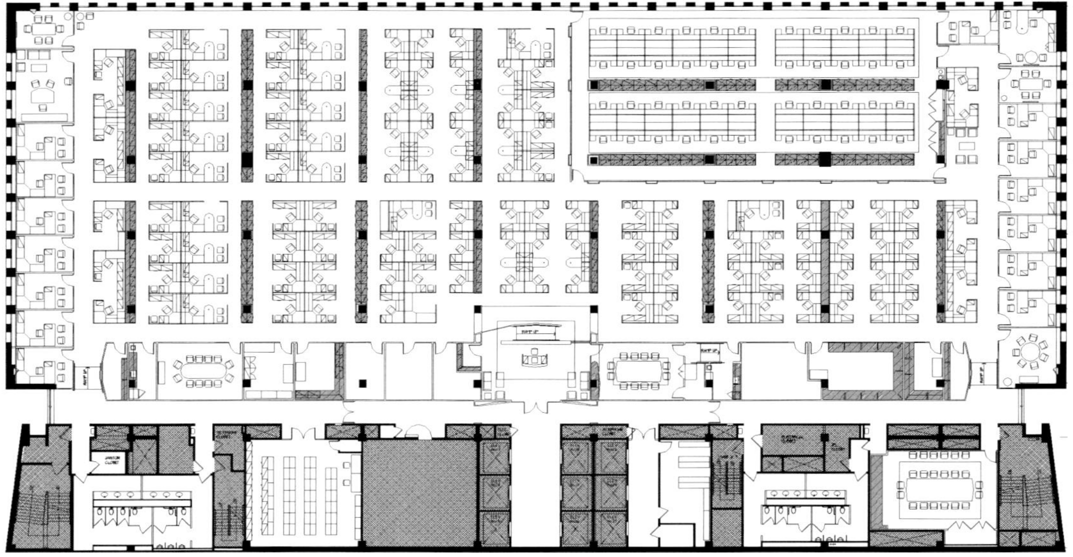

Detail of furniture layout.

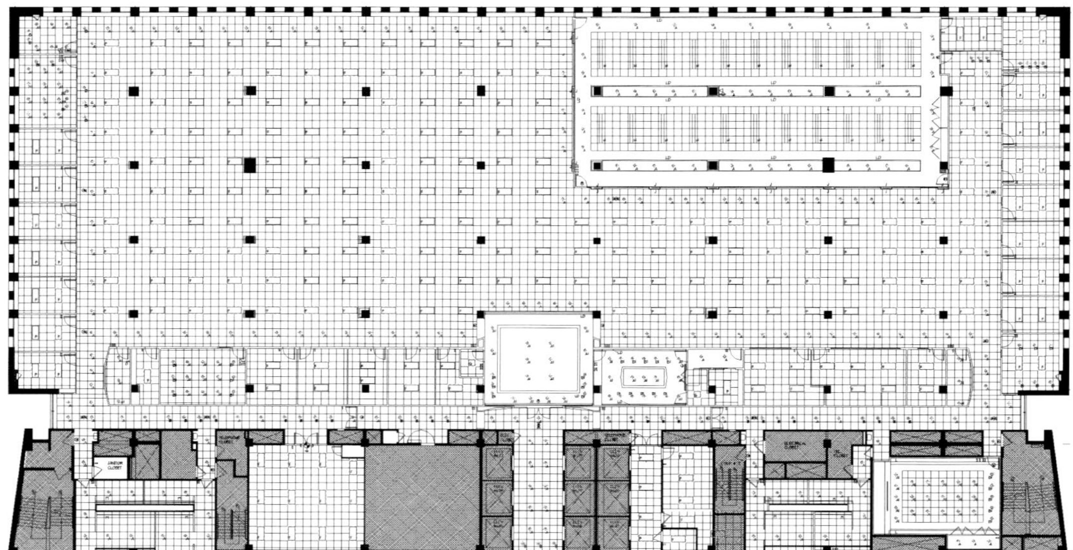

Detail of reflected ceiling plan.

The glass wall opens the main trading floor to view, but ensures traders can operate without disturbance from visitors.

Typical conference room centers on a table fully equipped to handle today's portable computer technology.

# Greenberg Traurig
## New York, New York 1998

Greenberg Traurig, the Florida-based law firm, commissioned The Switzer Group, Inc. to design a small sub-leased space for several employees at 399 Park Avenue. In 1995, The Switzer Group, Inc. designed the law firm's larger premises in Citicorp Center. In 1998, Greenburg Traurig commissioned The Switzer Group, Inc. yet again, to design an 82,000-square-foot office space, on two and a half floors, in the Met Life building.

The location, however desirable, posed significant layout problems given floor plates in the shape of a diamond: each floor has a large central core and a long linear perimeter with huge columns set in a straight line down the middle of the existing corridors. Part of the solution involved using the columns as a design element and featuring them by widening the corridors, rounding the columns and adding decorative wall treatments.

Greenberg Traurig's staff consists of share holders, associates, paralegals and secretarial staff. The decision was made to implement the traditional law office configuration—i.e., lawyers' offices directly adjacent to secretaries for ease of communication. The designers devised a standardized distribution of space, establishing a clear hierarchy by instituting a ratio of square feet per attorney with three basic office types: corner offices, with three windows each, were reserved for shareholders; associates offices included two windows each; room was also determined for secretarial stations and supervisory personnel.

Specialties are separated by floor, with the litigation division and law library on 14, the real estate division on 15 and additional support offices on 16. The overall space also includes a training room, lunchroom and pantry, storage, word processing area, accounting division, and a conference center, as well as separate conference rooms dispersed throughout the entire plan. Divider walls in the main conference room allow for the creation of one large or three smaller spaces. The entire facility is networked. Except for mahogany paneling set over windows and desk fronts, the designers used painted surfaces rather than millwork and workstations rather than custom furnishings.

A glass enclosure surrounds the interior stair.

E evator lobby and reception area.

Typical elevator section and details.

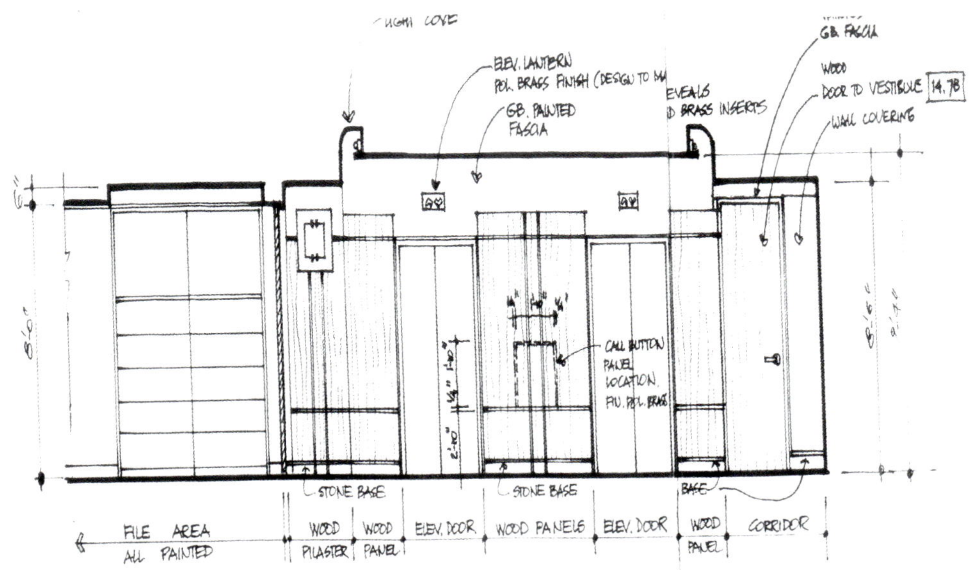

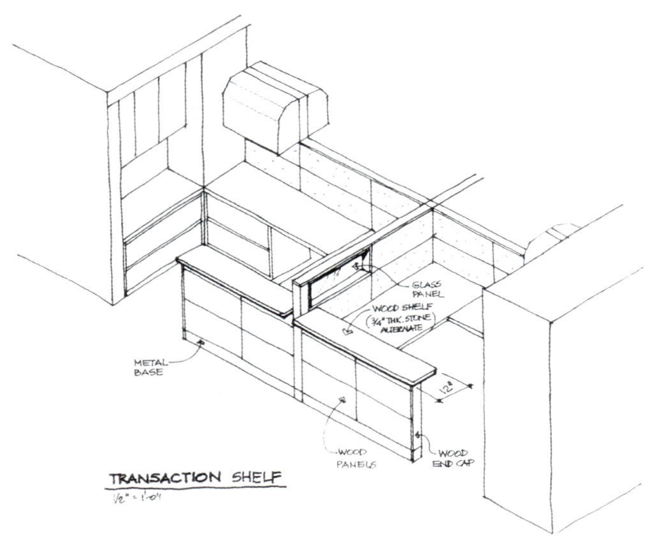

GLASS PANEL
WOOD SHELF (3/4" THK. STONE ALTERNATE)
METAL BASE
WOOD PANELS
WOOD END CAP
12"
TRANSACTION SHELF
1/2" = 1'-0"


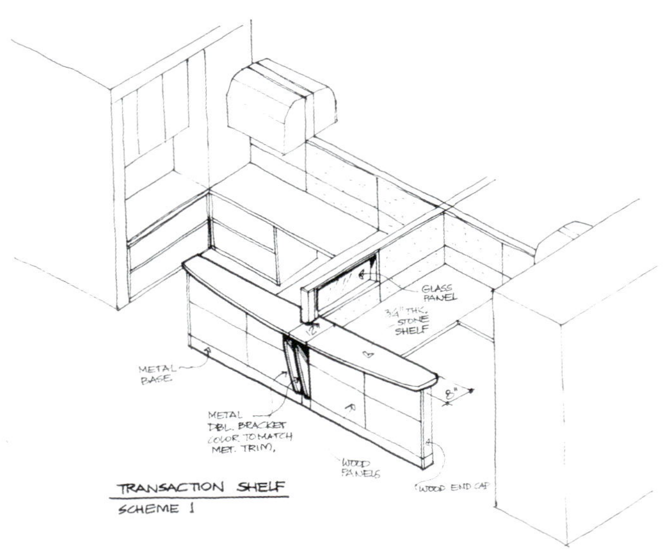

GLASS PANEL
3/4" THK. STONE SHELF
METAL BASE
METAL DBL. BRACKET COLOR TO MATCH MET. TRIM.
WOOD PANELS
WOOD END CAP
12"
8"
TRANSACTION SHELF
SCHEME 1

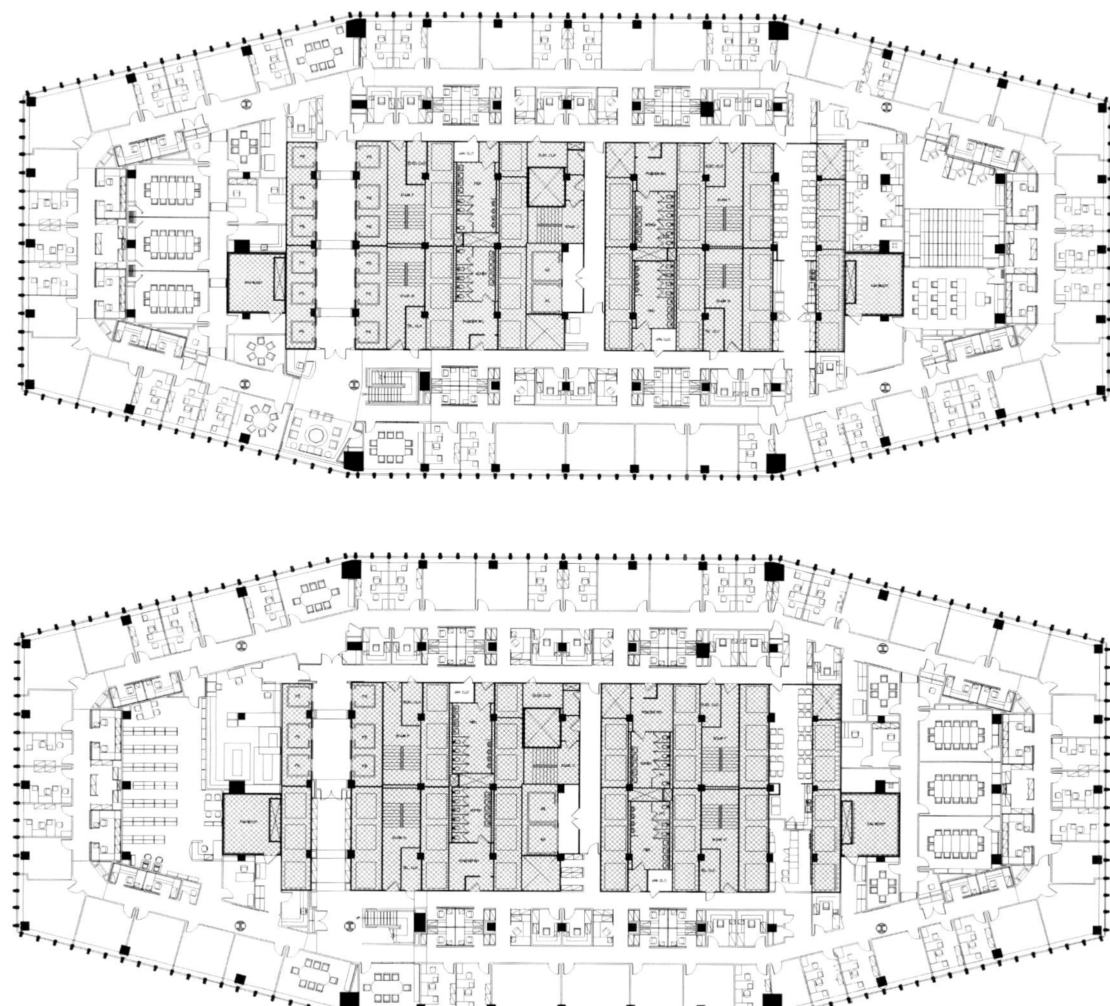

Opposite, clockwise from top
left: Reception; Open-plan
space for support staff;
Senior Partner's office with
three windows; Law library.

Floor plan for 15th floor.

Two versions of secretarial
support stations.

Floor plan for 14th floor.

# Design as an Understanding of the Business Environment:

# Pfizer, Inc.
## New York, New York 1999

Pfizer, Inc. commissioned The Switzer Group, Inc. to design a 60,000-square-foot corporate training-and-dining facility at the concourse level of 150 East 42nd Street. The program included a gallery with a rotating art collection and food kiosks, conference center with conference, training and meeting rooms as well as a dividable 200-seat multi-purpose room and breakout areas, two private dining rooms, full service kitchen and servery, 320-seat corporate dining room, and back office space with data center, contractor storage, mail and reproduction center, offices and maintenance.

The gallery acts as the facility's hub. Reached via stairs or escalator, it provides a common meeting and greeting area for Pfizer, Inc. employees as well as direct access to the dining wing and office space on the left and the meeting and training areas on the right. Materials throughout are durable, and include terrazzo flooring in high traffic areas, stainless steel, different qualities of glass and woven stainless steel wrapped over plywood panels for art display. Figured makare paneling extends throughout the interior.

Because the entire facility is windowless, the designers employed a palette of translucent and reflective materials to create an interior glow. Laminated wire glass diffusers over ceiling fixtures create luminous planes above the servery and kiosks. A backlit alabaster wall fronts the private dining rooms, which double as informal meeting spaces.

A reception area and concierge station provide entry to the suite of meeting and training rooms, which adjust in size via operable partitions. A large center room has a 20-foot ceiling and features rear projection, a combination of fluorescent cove lighting and incandescent downlighting. Plaster walls enclose conference rooms sporting cove lighting and metal ceilings with recessed MR16 fixtures.

A large cylindrical form marks the entrance to the servery and dining area, which locks off at night. The servery includes reflective and sparkling elements: an aluminum ceiling, low-voltage cable lighting, glass mosaic tiles, black granite, and custom finished stainless steel surfaces. The dining area features integral-color plaster walls, crackle glass and incandescent lighting. Chairs are stackable, and none of the seating is fixed.

Conference center training room.

Entry to the gallery lined with woven, stainless steel wrapped panels.

A large, cylindrical
glass form marks the
entry to the servery.

Conference break area.

Private dining areas are placed behind an alabaster wall, across the aisle from the cafeteria.

A wood-paneled corridor leads from the dining center to the training center.

The 320-seat corporate dining room can be divided into smaller, more intimate spaces or used for private receptions. Alabaster panels were used to give this room the illusion of natural light.

The actual floor layout of the dining room and training and support facilities.

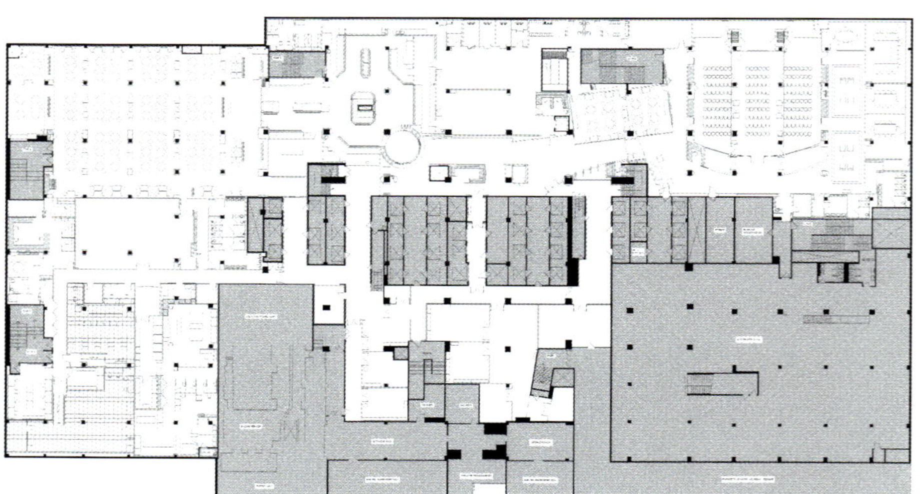

The servery incorporates a number of reflective materials to add visual interest to the interior.

Crackle glass, custom-finished steel and mosaic tiles are highlights of the materials' palette.

An aluminum ceiling, low-voltage lighting, integral-color plaster walls and a patterned carpet are the servery's primary design elements.

Design as an
Understanding
of the Business
Environment:

# Western International Media
## New York, New York 1999

This Los Angeles-based electronic media company commissioned The Switzer Group, Inc. to redesign its newly expanded New York headquarters. The designers worked with the client's facilities group and president to create a new image and to implement it in 15,500 square feet of space. The program delineated the need for two conference rooms and a president's office with adjacent conference space, reception area and workstations for the rest of the staff.

The designers reused the existing workstations, eliminating doors to create a sense of openness and volume. Contrasting colors and materials were employed to create interesting variations of textures and forms. The design begins in the elevator lobby, which establishes the color palette used within the space. Elevator walls and doors feature an encaustic finish. Concrete tiles pave the lobby and reception area floors. Lighting has been dimmed to a cozy level.

The reception area continues the themes established at the entry. The desk is constructed of inexpensive materials—stained particle board and MDF—used in an unusual manner. An encaustic material covers the wall behind the reception desk. Another wall is punctured by backlit elements that simulate windows, a device that camouflages the view. Wall washers accent the reception wall, intensifying the color and drawing attention to the desk. Downlights are used throughout. The designers developed center/center pivot doors to articulate the entries of both the large and the small conference rooms.

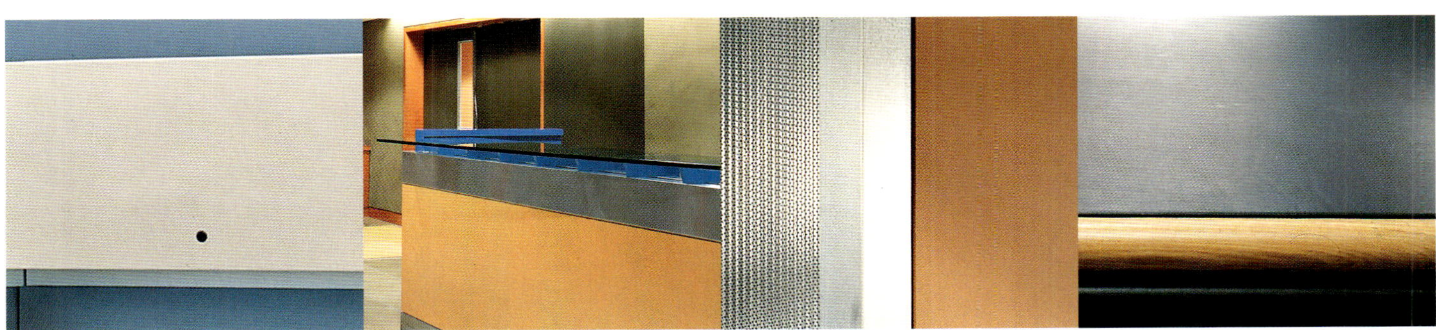

Concrete paving tiles establish the strong color palette
used throughout the interior. An encaustic-finished wall backs
the custom reception desk.

Corrugated metal walls add
interest to the corridor.

Center/center pivot doors open into a large, wood-paneled conference room fully equipped for the demands of today's technology.

An executive office is en suite with the small conference room.

Support staff cubicle.

Design as an
Understanding
of the Business
Environment:

# Phillips-
# Van Heusen
## New York, New York 1999

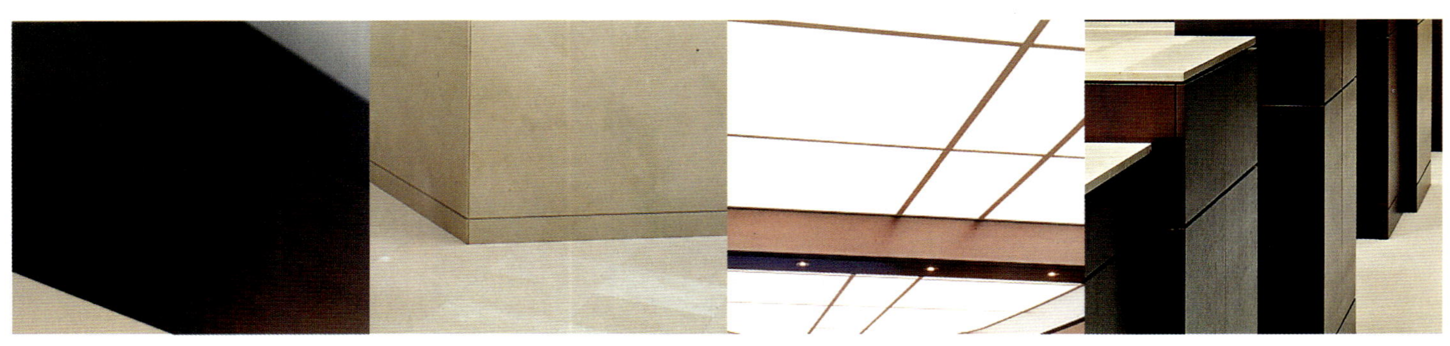

The Switzer Group, Inc. recently completed 18,000 square feet of executive
space at 200 Madison Avenue for Phillips-Van Heusen, a large, publicly held company in the fashion
industry. The client, which owns a number of clothing lines and licenses some well-known brands, had
decided to consolidate two existing locations in ten floors at this site, of which the executive floor was
one. The designers were asked to create a corporate floor that projected an image suitable to the industry
the company and its officers. The program for the executive floor included eight private offices with
various seating options, private restrooms and adjacent conference suites, workspaces for the administrative staff, a boardroom and pantry facilities.

Private offices—including those for the chairman, president, vice chairman, investment relations
officer, chief financial officer and chief counsel—were designed along the perimeter of the floor. Eight
custom-built workstations with polished stone transaction counters were constructed for the administrative staff. Oversized office doors, a vaulted wood ceiling, hand-finished, mahogany stained cherry
paneled walls and creme marble floors are among the details.

The chairman and the president have different sensibilities. Each is clearly expressed in this individual office suite. The chairman's office features very traditional appointments, with an antique partner s
desk and fine antique reproduction pieces. The president's office tends to the modern end of the design
spectrum, with sleek Italian furnishings sporting leather tops and marble details. The shell of the interior
is encased in custom millwork with no moldings in the traditional sense; the lines of the panels are clean,
providing an elegant envelope for the occupants. Artwork and occasional pieces of furniture provide a
smooth transition among the private spaces.

A vaulted wood ceiling tops the beautifully styled waiting room.

The skylight of the chairman's private conference area sheds light on the custom millwork and traditional furnishings that appoint the space.

Reception area
with skylight.

Support and administrative staff occupy custom-built workstations
with polished stone transaction counters.

The reception area features a vaulted wood ceiling, custom millwork on walls, oversized
doors to conference and office spaces and traditional furnishings.

The executive boardroom is
also wood paneled.

Leather-topped Italian designs and marble details lend the president's office a contemporary style.

The antiques and reproductions in the chairman's office are evidence of a more traditional style.

By contrast, the reproductions and antiques within the interior shown here exemplify the chairman's preference.

# Credits

**The Equitable, Re-deployment, various projects**

The Equitable, Life Insurance Group, 2 Penn Plaza New York 1986
PROJECT TEAM:
Lou Switzer, Chairman/CEO—Project Principal
Robert T. Sutter, AIA—Project Manager
John W. Rose, Jr.—Project Manager
George Romanella—Design Director
Marilyn Richter—Project Designer
K. Nandoo—Technical Coordinator
SOURCES:
SYSTEMS FURNITURE Knoll
GENERAL CONTRACTOR Structure Tone, Inc.
FOOD SERVICE Beer Associates
MEP ENGINEER Gleit Engineering Group
PHOTOGRAPHED BY Peter Paige

The Equitable, Corporate Operations Group, 40 Rector Street, New York 1984
PROJECT TEAM:
Lou Switzer, Chairman/CEO—Project Principal
John W. Rose, Jr.—Project Manager
Jack Travis—Project Designer
SOURCES:
SYSTEMS FURNITURE Westinghouse

The Equitable, Investment Management Corporation, 1221 Avenue of the Americas, New York 1986
PROJECT TEAM:
Lou Switzer, Chairman/CEO—Project Principal
Robert Kellogg—Project Manager
Marilyn Richter—Project Designer
SOURCES:
SYSTEMS FURNITURE Kimball
PHOTOGRAPHED BY Mark Ross

Fiat USA, Inc., New York 1989
PROJECT TEAM:
Lou Switzer, Chairman/CEO—Project Principal
Joseph Mancuso—Design Director
K. Nandoo—Technical Coordinator
SOURCES:
MILLWORK Craftsman Woodworking Inc.
FURNITURE Systems-Teknion
GENERAL CONTRACTOR AJ Contracting
PHOTOGRAPHED BY Christopher Lovi

Bidermann Industries USA, Inc., New York 1989
PROJECT TEAM:
Lou Switzer, Chairman/CEO—Project Principal
Joan Peterson—Project Manager
Stewart Fishbein, RA—Project Coordinator
Christopher Leary, RA—Project Designer
Steven Smith—Technical Coordinator
PHOTOGRAPHED BY Brian T. McNally

Integrated Resources, Inc., New York 1989
PROJECT TEAM:
Lou Switzer, Chairman/CEO—Project Principal
Robert T. Sutter, AIA—Project Manager
Stewart Fishbein, RA—Project Manager
Joseph Mancuso, RA—Design Director
Paul Boley—Designer

Adrienne Cartelli—Designer
Carmel Sherman—Designer
Janet Goldman—Designer
Joan Peterson—Technical Director
K. Nandoo—Technical Coordinator
Charles Poblete—Senior Technician
SOURCES:
CARPET TILE Milliken/Mort West Mills
WORKSTATION Herman Miller, Inc. Ethospace
WORKSTATION SEATING Herman Miller, Inc.
FILES Herman Miller, Inc.
PAINT Benjamin Moore
OFFICE FRONTS Herman Miller, Inc.
FOOD SERVICE CONSULTANT Cini-Little International
MEP ENGINEERS Robert Derector Engineers, Syska & Hennessey, Engineers
GENERAL CONTRACTOR Gotham/NICO Joint Venture
PHOTOGRAPHED BY Mark Ross

EMI Music Worldwide, New York 1992
PROJECT TEAM:
Lou Switzer, Chairman/CEO—Project Principal
Michael Mazzella—Project Manager
Joseph Mancuso, RA—Design Director
Gregory Switzer, RA—Project Designer
Daniel McCarthy—Project Designer
Phil Ebalarosa—Technical Director
Walter Leute—Technical Coordinator
SOURCES:
CARPET Hokanson
WORKSTATIONS, FILES Unifor
FURNITURE Dakota Jackson/David Saunders, Association/Vitra/Stow Davis, Davis/Brickel/Knoll/B&B Italia, Michael Bernstein Designs
MILLWORK L. Vaughn Co.
WINDOW TREATMENTS Contour Drapery
AUDIO/VISUAL Audio Video Systems
PHOTOGRAPHED BY Durston Saylor

New Charlston Capital Management, New York 1992
PROJECT TEAM:
Lou Switzer, Chairman/CEO
Donald A. Sachar—Project Principal
Elanora Krupka, RA—Project Manager
Walter Leute—Project Coordinator
Joseph Mancuso—Design Director
Paul Boley—Designer
Walter Leute—Technical Coordinator
SOURCES:
MILLWORK Pilot Woodworking
WINDOW TREATMENT Contour Drapery
MEP ENGINEERS Cosentini Consulting Engineers
GENERAL CONTRACTOR Lehr Construction
CONSULTING ENGINEER M. Chetrit Engineers
PHOTOGRAPHED BY Mark Ross

Chase Manhattan Bank, MetroTech Center, New York 1993
PROJECT TEAM:
Lou Switzer, Chairman/CEO
Robert T. Sutter, AIA—Project Principal
Richard Kline—Project Manager
Steven Rowland—Project Manager

Joseph Mancuso, RA—Design Director
Paul Boley—Designer
Mark Oliver, RA—Technical Coordinator
Charles Poblete—Senior Technician
SOURCES:
SYSTEMS FURNITURE Knoll
GENERAL CONTRACTOR Lehrer McGovern Bovis, Inc.
PHOTOGRAPHED BY Robert Thien

Consolidated Edison Company Of New York, Inc., New York 1993
PROJECT TEAM:
Lou Switzer, Chairman/CEO
Robert T. Sutter, AIA—Project Principal
Stewart Fishbein, RA—Project Manager
Michael Mazzela, RA—Project Manager
J. Daniel Mrozek, RA—Design Manager
Carmel Sherman—Designer
Andrew Mascia—Field Manager
Walter Leute—Technical Coordinator
Charles Poblete—Senior Technician
Qurban Hussain—Assistant Field Manager
SOURCES:
CARPET The Carpet Group
TERRAZZO FLOOR D. Magnan
STONE FLOOR Wilkinson
TABLES Howe Furniture, Corporation/Johnson/ Knoll "Z" tables
CHAIRS/MEETING & CAFETERIA Gunlocke
WORKSTATIONS All-Steel
WORKSTATION SEATING All-Steel/Knoll
RECEPTION DESKS Custom
FILES All-Steel/Knoll
PAINT Benjamin Moore
LUNCH ROOM SEATING Gunlocke
FOOD SERVICE DESIGN Beer Associates
EXHIBIT DESIGNER (LOBBY & ARCADE) Edwin Scholossberg, Inc.
OFFICE FRONTS ACME/Kawneer
LIGHTING DESIGN Hayden McKay Lighting Design
UPHOLSTERY Maharam/Knoll
WALL COVERING Maharam
AUDIO/VISUAL Smith Meeker Engineering
HARDWOOD VISUAL Lectern
MEP ENGINEER Joseph R. Loring Associates, Inc.
STRUCTURAL ENGINEER The Office of Irwin G. Cantor, PC
CORE/SHELL ARCHITECTS May Whitelaw & Pinska
LANDSCAPE ARCHITECT Coe Lee Robinson Roesch, Inc.
CONTRACTOR Herbert Construction Company
PHOTOGRAPHED BY Peter Paige

IBM, Regional Headquarters, New Jersey 1993-94
PROJECT TEAM:
Lou Switzer, Chairman/CEO
Elizabeth Holechek—Project Principal
Steven Hargis, RA—Project Manager
Frank Wiechnik—Designer
Neville Lewis—Design Consultant
SOURCES:
CARPET Milliken Carpet/Interface
WORKSTATION CHAIRS, FILES All-Steel
CONFERENCE TABLE Steelcase/Partnership
PLASTIC LAMINATES Formica Corporation
LIGHTING DESIGN Horton-Lees Lighting Design

**LIGHTING** Abolite (Stem-Held Industrials In Open Area)
**DOWN-LIGHTS** Kurt Versen
**FLUORESCENT UP-LIGHTS** Linear Lighting
**GENERAL CONTRACTOR** Structure Tone, Inc.
**PHOTOGRAPHED BY** Peter Paige

Westinghouse Broadcasting, New York 1995
**PROJECT TEAM:**
Lou Switzer, Chairman/CEO
Mark Oliver, RA—Project Manager
J. Daniel Mrozek, RA—Design Manager
Walter Leute—Technical Coordinator
**SOURCES:**
**ARTWORK CONSULTANT** Ann Alter
**STONE** Port Morris
**MILLWORK** RIMI Woodworking
**ENGINEERS** M. Chetrit Engineers
**LEATHER** Spinneybeck Leather
**TEXTILES** Lee Jofa/Knoll
**LIGHTING** Stan Deutche
**CARPET** Bently
**GENERAL CONTRACTORS** Structure Tone, Inc.
**FURNITURE/WORKSTATIONS** Knoll/Bernhardt/Dongia
**18TH CENTURY JAPANESE SCREEN** NAGA Antiques, Ltd.
**PHOTOGRAPHED BY** Paul Warchol

Citibank, NA, New York 1991
**PROJECT TEAM:**
Lou Switzer, Chairman/CEO
Beth Holechek—Project Principal
Mark Oliver—Project Manager
J. Daniel Mrozek, RA—Design Manager
Walter Leute—Technical Coordinator
Charles Poblete—Senior Technician
Christian Stefanescu—Technical Coordinator
**SOURCES:**
**MEP ENGINEERING** Meyer Strong & Jones
**PHOTOGRAPHED BY** Paul Warchol

The Equitable, 1290 Avenue of the Americas, New York 1997
**PROJECT TEAM:**
Lou Switzer, Chairman/CEO
Robert T. Sutter, AIA—Project Principal
Stewart Fishbein, RA—Project Manager
Gerald Silver—Project Manager
J. Daniel Mrozek, RA—Design Manager
Kyra Saulnier—Designer
Maura Sordo—Designer
Vincent Nealy—Designer
Amy Gallagher—Designer
Walter Leute—Technical Coordinator
Charles Poblete—Technical Coordinator
Christian Stefanescu—Technical Coordinator
Gus David—Technician
**SOURCES:**
**CARPET TILE** Bentley
**LIGHTING** Kurt Versen/Belfer/Edison Price
**CEILING** Louis Poulsen/Baldinger
**WALL** American Glass Light Co.
**TASK** Herman Miller, Inc.
**LINEAR LIGHTING** Ambient/Switzer Group (Custom)

**ACOUSTICAL CONSULTANT** Robert A. Hanson
**FLOORING** Bentley/Edwards Fields
**BROADLOOM** Mannington Commercial
**VINYL** Armstrong/While Oak Natural
**WOOD** Estre
**TILE** American Olean
**EXECUTIVE CHAIRS** Geiger Brickel
**LEATHER CHAIR** Edelman Leather
**FILES (HIGH DENSITY)** Modern Office—Spacesaver
**PAINT** Benjamin Moore
**WORKSTATIONS** Herman Miller, Inc.
**WORKSTATION CHAIRS** Haworth, Inc.
**DESK/CREDENZA/DESK CHAIR/TABLE** Council
**DESK/CREDENZA/TABLE** Berhardt Contract Furniture
**DESK CHAIR/VISITOR CHAIR** Geiger Brickel
**CONFERENCE TABLE** Wall Goldfinger
**VISITOR CHAIRS** Smith Watson/Charles McMurray
**ARCHITECTURAL WOODWORK** Nordic Interiors, Inc.
**GLASS** Benheim/Pearlstein
**BOARDROOM WALL COVERINGS** Scalamandre
**WINDOW TREATMENTS** Levolor/Solar Shade/Mecho Shade
**WALL COVERINGS** DesignTex/Carnegie
**WALL GUARDS** Acrovyn
**FABRIC PANELS** Maharam/Jack Lanor Larson
**CEILINGS** Armstrong
**WORKSTATIONS** Herman Miller, Inc.
**AUDIO/VISUAL CONSULTANTS** Cerami & Associates
**MEP ENGINEER** Edwards & Zuck
**STRUCTURAL ENGINEER** Cantor/Seinuk Group
**SECURITY** Electronic System Associates
**RELOCATION CONSULTANT** Kelly, Legan & Gerard, Inc.
**PROJECT MANAGEMENT CONSULTANTS** Bennis + Reissman
**CONSTRUCTION MANAGER** Lehrer McGovern Bovis, Inc.
**FURNITURE CONSULTANT** Ferguson, Cox Associates
**PHOTOGRAPHED BY** Peter Paige

Forstmann & Company, New York 1999
**PROJECT TEAM:**
Lou Switzer, Chairman/CEO
Louis Villafane—Project Principal
Gary Schmidt—Project Manager
Gregory Gresham, RA—Design Manager
Joseph Calpo-Riveria—Senior Designer
Maura Sordo—Designer
Maryse Livoti—Designer
Damon Gray—Technical Coordinator
**SOURCES:**
**CARPET** Patrick Carpet
**SLATE FLOOR (STONE SOURCE)** Lotus Slate/Absolute Black Granite
**CONFERENCE TABLES** Existing
**CONFERENCE SEATING** Existing
**WORKSTATIONS** Knoll/Reff
**WORKSTATION SEATING** Existing
**RECEPTION SEATING** Existing
**RECEPTION DESK** Custom Millwork
**RECEPTION TABLE** Existing
**FILES** Existing
**PAINT** Benjamin Moore
**LUNCH ROOM** Existing
**LUNCH ROOM SEATING** Existing
**OFFICE FRONTS** ACME
**GLASS** Clear Glass

**LIGHTING** Rambush/NeoRay/Spero
**UPHOLSTERY** Pollack & Associates
**VINYL FLOORING** Lonplate
**VCT** Armstrong
**MEP ENGINEER** G.C. Eng. & Associates
**STRUCTURAL ENGINEER** Thorston-Thomassetti
**GENERAL CONTRACTOR** Tishman Construction
**PHOTOGRAPHED BY** Cervin Robinson

Allen & Overy, New York 1998
**PROJECT TEAM:**
Lou Switzer, Chairman/CEO
Robert T. Sutter, AIA—Project Principal
Gregory Gresham, RA—Design Manager
Maura Sordo—Designer
Julius Victoria—Technical Coordinator
**SOURCES:**
**CARPET** Interface/Bentley Mills, Inc.
**PAINT** Benjamin Moore
**CONFERENCE TABLES** Wall Goldfinger
**RECEPTION SEATING** Charles McMurray Designs
**CONFERENCE ROOMS** Knoll
**PRIVATE OFFICES** Harter
**WORKSTATIONS** Geiger Brickel
**VERTICAL FILES** Meridian
**LIGHT FIXTURES** NeoRay/Artemide
**LIGHT CONSULTANTS** NeoRay/Artemide
**UPHOLSTERY** Spinneybeck
**LEATHER** Sina Pearson Designers/Harter
**WALL COVERING** ICF-Unika Vaev-Niemkamper-Helikon/ Pollack& Associates
**WOOD PANELING** Caccamo Woodworking Corp.
**MEP ENGINEER** A.G. Consulting Engineers
**GENERAL CONTRACTOR** Structure Tone, Inc.
**PHOTOGRAPHED BY** Cervin Robinson

Chase Manhattan Bank, Securities Lending Facility, New York 1998
**PROJECT TEAM:**
Lou Switzer, Chairman/CEO
Louis Villafane—Project Principal
Gregory Gresham, RA—Project Designer
Wendy McClung—Designer
George Cho—Technical Coordinator
**SOURCES:**
**CARPET** Mannington
**FURNITURE** Steelcase Paul Brayton/Vecta
**CONFERENCE TABLES** Custom/Nordic Interiors, Inc.
**WORKSTATIONS** Steelcase
**WORKSTATION SEATING** Steelcase
**RECEPTION SEATING** Paul Brayton
**RECEPTION DESKS** Custom/Nordic Interiors, Inc.
**RECEPTION TABLES** Paul Brayton
**FILES** Steelcase
**PAINT** Benjamin Moore
**OFFICES FRONTS** ACME
**GLASS** Bendheim
**LIGHTING** NeoRay/Lightolier
**PLASTIC LAMINATES** Neuxman Pionite
**WALLING COVERING** Carnegie/DesignTEX
**WOOD PANELING** Nordic Interior, Inc.
**AUDIO/VISUAL** Smith Meeker Engineering
**MEF ENGINEERS** Joseph R. Loring & Associates, Inc./

Lilker Associates
**GENERAL CONTRACTOR** J.G. Kennedy
**PHOTOGRAPHED BY** Peter Paige

Greenberg Traurig, New York 1998
**PROJECT TEAM:**
Lou Switzer, Chairman/CEO
Louis Villafane—Project Principal
Gregory Gresham, RA—Design Manager
Maura Sordo—Designer
Wendy McClung—Designer
George Cho—Technical Coordinator
**SOURCES:**
**CARPET** Shaw/Harbinger
**STONE FLOOR (MARBLE)** Hauteville/Aegean Brown/Noir Saint
Laurent
**CONFERENCE TABLES** Wall Goldfinger
**CONFERENCE ROOM SEATING** Bright
**OFFICE GUEST SEATING FABRIC** Textus
**GUEST CHAIRS** Gunlocke
**WORKSTATIONS** Knoll/Reff
**WORKSTATIONS SEATING** Steelcase
**RECEPTION DESK** Custom Millwork/Nordic Interiors, Inc.
**RECEPTION TABLE** Zographos
**FILES** Meridian
**PAINT** Benjamin Moore
**LUNCH ROOM TABLES** Johnson
**LUNCH ROOM CHAIRS** Harter, Inc.
**LIGHTING** Zumtobel/Kurt Versen National/Belfer
**UPHOSTERY** DesignTex/Gilford
**WALLCOVERING** Jack Lenor
**LEATHER** Bernhardt Contract Furniture
**REFINISH/REUPHOLSTER** Thomas Amato and Sons
**SIGNAGE** Dale Travis Associates
**FOOD SERVICE** Restaurant Marketing Associates
**FURNITURE** Empire Furniture/Arenson Office
Furnishings/Camilo Furniture
**WORKSTATIONS** Knoll/Reff
**RECEPTION SEATING** Bernhardt Contract Furniture
**TELECOMMUNICATIONS** Windmill Communications, Inc.
**PLASTIC LAMINATES** Nevamar
**WALL COVERING** Gilford/DeisgnTex/Jack Lenor Larsen
**WOOD PANELING** Nordic Interior, Inc.
**MEP ENGINEERS** Edwards and Zuck, P.C.
**STRUCTURAL ENGINEER** Severud Associates
**GENERAL CONTRACTOR** Lehr Construction Corp.
**PHOTOGRAPHED BY** Cervin Robinson

Pfizer, Inc., New York City 1999
**PROJECT TEAM:**
Lou Switzer, Chairman/CEO
Robert T. Sutter, AIA—Project Principal
Stewart Fishbein, RA—Project Manager
Gregory Gresham, RA—Design Manager
Elanor Lasky—Designer
Maryse Livoti—Designer
Walter Leute—Technical Coordinator
Charles Poblete—Senior Technician
Julius Victoria—Senior Technician
Jose Vasquez—Technician
**SOURCES:**
**CARPET** Hokanson, Inc./Masland Contract/
The Harbinger Co./Shaw, Terrazzo/Granite/Alabaster,

Port Morris Tile & Marble
**CUSTOM MILLWORK** Nordic Interiors, Inc.
**WOVEN STAINLESS STEEL AND COLUMNS** Mison Concepts, Inc.
**CUSTOM GLASS** John Depp, Inc.
**LIGHTING** Edison Price/Reggiani Lighting/Elliptipar/
Various Others
**PAINT** Benjamin Moore
**ENCAUSTIC PLASTER** Amian Group, Inc.
**FABRIC PANELS** Knoll (Textiles)
**CONFERENCE TABLES** Wall Goldfinger, Inc.
**CONFERENCE/MEETING ROOM SEATING** Herman Miller, Inc./Davis
**FURNITURE** Industries, Inc.
**LOUNGE SEATING & TABLES** Bernhardt Contract Furniture
**FOOD SERVICE CONSULTANT** Romano Gatland
**LUNCH ROOM TABLES** Johnson Industries
**LUNCH ROOM SEATING** Davis Furniture Industries, Inc.
**SECURITY CONSULTANT** Security Management Systems, Inc.
**UPHOLSTERY** Paul Brayton Designs
**LEATHER** Edelman Leather/Spinneybeck
**WORKSTATIONS/SEATING/& FILES** Haworth, Inc.
**AUDIO/VISUAL** Shen Milsom Wilke
**ACOUSTICAL CONSULTANT** Shen Milsom Wilke
**MEP ENGINEER** Syska & Hennessy, Inc.
**GENERAL CONTRACTOR** Lehrer McGovern & Bovis, Inc.
**PHOTOGRAPHED BY** Cervin Robinson

Western International Media, New York 1998
**PROJECT TEAM:**
Lou Switzer, Chairman/CEO
Louis Villafane—Project Principal
Joseph Calpo-Rivera—Design Manager
Maura Sordo—Designer
Walter Leute—Technical Coordinator
Damon Gray—Technician
**SOURCES:**
**CARPET** Brooklyn Carpet Exchange
**FURNITURE** Unisource Office Services
**HIGH DENSITY SYSTEM** Modern Office Systems
**STONE FLOOR** Concrete The Get Real
**CONFERENCE TABLES** Haworth, Inc.
**WORKSTATIONS** Haworth, Inc.—Premise System
**WORKSTATION SEATING** Haworth, Inc.
**RECEPTION SEATING** Bernhardt Contract Furniture
**RECEPTION TABLE** Bernhardt Contract Furniture
**RECEPTION DESK** Custom-Handan Architectural Millworker
**FILES** Haworth, Inc.
**PAINT** Benjamin Moore
**LUNCH ROOM** Haworth, Inc.
**LUNCH ROOM SEATING** Haworth, Inc.
**OFFICE FRONTS** Haworth, Inc.
**LIGHTING** Ledanite
**UPHOLSTERY** Ledaute/Zumtobel/Knoll (Textiles)/Donghia
Telecommunications, Rockefeller Group Tele Services, Inc.
**PLASTIC LAMINATE** Abet Laminati/Formica Corporation
**MEP ENGINEER** Jack Stone & Associates
**STRUCTURAL ENGINEER** Thorton-Tomasetti/Engineers
**GENERAL CONTRACTOR** Alexander Wolf & Sons
**PHOTOGRAPHED BY** Cervin Robinson

Phillips-Van Heusen, New York 1999
**PROJECT TEAM:**
Lou Switzer, Chairman/CEO
Louis Villafane—Project Principal

J. Daniel Mrozek, RA—Design Manager
Joseph Calpo-Riveria—Design Manager
Nancy Pearson—Designer
Maryse Livoti—Designer
Walter Leute—Technical Coordinator
Hank Pena—Technician
**SOURCES:**
**CARPET** Edward Fields
**MARBLE FLOOR** Worldwide Marble Corp. Material
**BOARDROOM TABLE** Wall Goldfinger, Inc.
**SEATING** HBF
**WORKSTATIONS** Custom-Patella Wood Working
**WORKSTATION SEATING** HBF/Holly Hunt
**RECEPTION SEATING** HBF/Holly Hunt
**RECEPTION/SECRETARIAL DESK** Amadeus/Padilla
**RECEPTION AREA RUG** Renaissance Carpet & Carpetries, Inc.
**STONE WORK** Amadeus
**LOUNGE AREA SEATING** Donghia/Holly Hunt/J. Robert Scott, Inc.
**LOUNGE AREA TABLES/CHESTS** Randolph & Hein/Nancy Corzine
**CHAIRMAN'S OFFICE FURNITURE** Smith & Watson/George Smith/
Mason-Art, Incorporated
**CHAIRMAN'S CONFERENCE ROOM** Smith & Watson
**MILLWORK** Patella Wood Working
**PRESIDENT'S OFFICE** Poltrona-Frau/ICF-Unika Vaev-
Niemkamper-Helikon/J. Robert Scott, Inc.
**PRESIDENT'S CONFERENCE ROOM** Poltrona-Frau/ICF-Unika Vaev-
Niemkamper-Helikon/J. Robert Scott, Inc.
**BOARDROOM LIGHTING** Custom by Switzer Group, Inc./Patella
Woodworking
**PAINT** Benjamin Moore
**GLASS** Custom by Switzer Group, Inc./Reggiani
**LIGHTING DESIGN** Syska & Hennessy, Inc.
**LIGHTING** Custom by Switzer Group, Inc./Reggiani
**AUDIO/VISUAL** SME
**LEATHER** Edelman Leather
**MEP ENGINEERS** Syska & Hennessy, Inc.
**GENERAL CONTRACTOR** Americon Construction & Consulting
**PROJECT MANAGER** S.A. Gavish, Inc.
**PHOTOGRAPHED BY** Cervin Robinson

# Acknowledgements

This book compiles the work of the Switzer Group, Inc. from its founding in 1975, to the present. None of these projects would have been successful without our talented architects and designers, the many engineers and consultants with whom we collaborated, and especially our clients who partnered with us in the creative process.

Thanks to the many people who contributed to the completion of this book. I would like to thank our architects and interior designers who prepared the drawings for this publication, our marketing staff who compiled project information, and the firm's principals who spent many hours preparing the project descriptions, reviewing the material and editing the text.

**Lou Switzer**

# The Switzer Group

EDIZIONI PRESS